The Unofficial Guide to Therapeutic Parenting for Childhood Aggression and Violence

by the same author

The Unofficial Guide to Adoptive Parenting
The Small Stuff, the Big Stuff and the Stuff In Between
Sally Donovan
Foreword by Dr Vivien Norris, Jim Clifford and Sue Clifford
ISBN 978 1 84905 536 9
eISBN 978 0 85700 959 3

The Unofficial Guide to Therapeutic Parenting – The Teen Years
Sally Donovan
Foreword by Dr Vivien Norris
ISBN 978 1 78592 174 2
eISBN 978 1 78450 444 1

No Matter What
An Adoptive Family's Story of Hope, Love and Healing
Sally Donovan
ISBN 978 1 84905 431 7
eISBN 978 0 85700 781 0

of related interest

Happy Families
A Parents' Guide to the Non-Violent Resistance Approach
Carmelite Avraham-Krehwinkel and David Aldridge
ISBN 978 1 84905 084 5
eISBN 978 0 85700 305 8

Therapeutic Parenting Essentials
Moving from Trauma to Trust
Sarah Naish, Sarah Dillon and Jane Mitchell
ISBN 978 1 78775 031 9
eISBN 978 1 78775 032 6

Child to Parent Violence and Abuse
Family Interventions with Non-Violent Resistance
Declan Coogan
ISBN 978 1 84905 711 0
eISBN 978 1 78450 231 7

The Unofficial Guide to
Therapeutic Parenting
for Childhood
Aggression and Violence

Sally Donovan
and Carly Kingswood

Jessica Kingsley Publishers
London and Philadelphia

First published in Great Britain in 2023 by Jessica Kingsley Publishers
An imprint of John Murray Press

I

Copyright © Sally Donovan and Carly Kingswood 2023

A CIP catalogue record for this title is available from the
British Library and the Library of Congress

ISBN 978 1 83997 011 5
eISBN 978 1 83997 010 8

Printed and bound in the United States by Integrated Books International

Jessica Kingsley Publishers' policy is to use papers that are natural,
renewable and recyclable products and made from wood grown in sustainable forests. The logging and manufacturing processes are expected to
conform to the environmental regulations of the country of origin.

Jessica Kingsley Publishers
Carmelite House
50 Victoria Embankment
London EC4Y 0DZ

www.jkp.com

John Murray Press
Part of Hodder & Stoughton Limited
An Hachette UK Company

Contents

Part 1 : What Are We Dealing With Here?

Part 2: Build Knowledge and Skills, Keep Safe and Maintain Boundaries

Part 3: Develop Strategies and Create an Environment for Reflection and Repair

Part 4: Influences and Specific Challenges

Part 5: Take Care of Yourself and Travel in Hope

About the Authors

Sally Donovan OBE is an award-winning writer and author of books about adoption, therapeutic parenting and trauma, for children and adults. She works in charity communications and lives in the south of England with her family.

Carly Kingswood began her career as a social worker in the field of child protection, including within the care system. She retrained as a play therapist, adding this to various roles in social work, therapy and assessment that worked around her family. Having developed an interest in attachment and trauma, she worked for four years at Catchpoint, an organization offering therapy specifically with fostered and adopted children, which enabled her to work with parents alongside their children and young people. She and her family also began fostering at this time, a journey that lasted for ten years.

She gained an MA in therapeutic fostering and adoption and began working fully independently in 2014 from a beautiful farm setting in south west England where she has practised dyadic developmental psychotherapy, supervision and therapeutic life story work for many years. Carly is a trainer in a wide range of issues relating to attachment, trauma, adoption, fostering and therapeutic parenting. *The Unofficial Guide to Therapeutic Parenting for Childhood Aggression and Violence* with Sally Donovan is her first book.

Introduction

Parenting, caring for and loving a child whose distress plays out in violence and aggression is not easy. It has to be one of the most conflicting, confusing, frightening and complicated domestic situations anyone can find themselves in.

And yet from the outside looking in, it can appear simple enough. Adults need to step up and take charge of children who are lacking in discipline. Violence and abuse should never be tolerated. 'I simply wouldn't allow it,' some may declare. But such declarations so often unravel on first contact. If the solutions were straightforward, there would be very little violence and aggression in the home.

The emerging evidence tells a different story – violent incidents enacted by children towards the adults with whom they live are on the rise. It could be that media exposure and connections facilitated by social media are encouraging parents to break cover, share their stories and report incidents to the police. Or that violent and aggressive behaviour in childhood is becoming more common. It's probably a bit of both, but what seems undeniable is that it is a growing problem and one which society is struggling both to come to terms with and to respond to. What is not true to say, by any measure, is that this generation of parents, grandparents, aunts, uncles, brothers, sisters and carers are a weak, permissive and unintelligent bunch, raising demanding and entitled children. It is wise to avoid such views and those who express them.

Throughout our guide, we refer to violence and aggression as manifestations of distress or trauma. Distress and trauma impact our whole beings – psychologically, biologically, emotionally and physically. And they can result from anything that has caused emotional overwhelm, which has either not been helpfully processed or has re-occurred over a period of time. For a child, this might include a parental divorce or separation, family conflict, bereavement, displacement, racism, some types of relational experiences, medical trauma, bullying, and developmental trauma including abuse and neglect. Children struggling with such issues can behave in traumatized ways, particularly when we, the adults in their lives, are stressed, dysregulated and disconnected too.

It is not usual to discuss challenging behaviours in terms of trauma and this is a leap of faith that many have to make before the behaviours and the suggested approaches and strategies start to make sense. If you are smarting at the notion that your child is acting out because they have experienced some trauma, this is entirely usual and all we ask is that you bear with us for at least a few chapters.

The term trauma covers a broad range of experiences, but we don't rank these on some kind of trauma scale. We won't dwell on whether the divorce was 'amicable' or the hospital stay was 'short', or whether whatever happened to your child took place when they were 'just a baby'. To look into another person's experience from the outside, and judge that it couldn't have been *that* bad, is dangerous territory to get into. (The key word here is 'judge'.) For those living with violence, the end result is the same: distress, dysregulation, lashing out, shame and isolation. We all come at situations and process them differently because we are messily and wonderfully human.

You may be venturing into our book burdened with regrets and shame. There will undoubtedly be situations that could have gone differently, things that shouldn't have been said or that should have been said, and such is the way with parenting, especially high-end parenting. We have to find a way of taking away the sting and framing our perceived 'failures' as useful experiences – situations we learned something important from. We are where we are and we are – all of us – doing our best with what we've got. This book is a shame-free zone, so cast aside your shame burdens if you can.

Although we have set out the basics of the science of trauma and behaviour, with some pointers for those who want to get further into this subject, this is above all a practical guide for anyone parenting and caring for a child whose distress spills out into violence and aggression. It is an appalling and devastating situation to be in. If you are in a state of utter exhaustion and frazzled hopelessness, please know that we have written our book with you in mind. We've included plenty of 'easy wins' and tips, along with the deeper knowledge needed to get to the root causes of violent behaviour. This book is meant to be used, so write all over its pages, underline the parts you want to go back to and bend back the corners of the most useful pages. Think of it as your travel guide.

If you are still in some doubt that what you really need is a book about parenting (perhaps some well-meaning person bought it for you), then we have one more perspective to offer. Parenting a distressed child is an extraordinary situation and it demands extraordinary parenting. The usual parenting that everyone else around us can get away with will not do. This is a specialist guide to specialist parenting.

There is both a science and an art to this high-end parenting. The science (what is going on in distressed bodies and the strategies and responses informed by this knowledge), and the art (the creative, real-time, real-life ways in which we learn to carry out these strategies and responses) are as important as each other.

The science helps us to make sense of what can seem like a huge and confusing mess. It can also provide some detachment from the mess and bring logic back into the room, when it so often goes missing. Knowing some of the science can also help us to welcome empathy back too. Empathy, which may seem so distant right now, will return. It is an essential glue in sticking family life back together.

The art is where we go from there – applying our knowledge and skills to respond creatively to ever-evolving situations. Children and adults don't operate with a set of identical algorithms, which is why we need the art. The art and the science have to go hand-in-hand.

The particular and unique set of skills that marries the latest neuroscience, research and theories with the nitty gritty of real life sounds an awful lot easier than it is in practice. This is why we encourage you to take care of yourself and to allow others to. You will have to be clever about prioritizing your wellbeing, fit it in when you can and know when to scale back on unnecessary commitments. This kind of deliberate and thoughtful parenting, which we refer to as therapeutic parenting, is difficult and rather unrelenting, but it bears fruit when nothing else does.

Sticking with a child who reacts to stress with violence and aggression is an act of quiet, determined heroism. It demands that parents and carers pick themselves up, dust themselves off, dry their eyes and try again, over and over. It also asks that they open themselves up to learn new ways of seeing, being and doing. Learning, in a state of extreme vulnerability, is a really big ask. So too is dredging up the courage to travel forward with hope. The treasure is found when you and your child emerge out of the hell hole, with your lives intact and the skills and relationship to pursue a future that isn't all about distress and violence. It won't be perfect, but it will be something to behold – your own domestic masterpiece.

Pathway to a Peaceful Home

Our book follows a rough path to help you get from frazzled and hopeless to empowered and hopeful, with quite a few diversions along the way. Parenting a distressed child is a deeply imperfect art and nowhere near as neat as this pathway appears, but it's good to start with a plan and to return to it every now and again.

- Build knowledge and skills and achieve some easy wins.

- Keep safe, avoid conflict and maintain boundaries.

- Address the root causes.

- Develop strategies and create an environment for reflection and repair.

- Network, network, network.

- Take care of yourself and travel in hope.

TIP
Keep a diary

Record the incidents of violence and aggression that take place in your home or, if applicable, at school or in other situations.

As far as you can, recount the incident from start to end, but don't worry if you jump around in time. Recall of stressful events can often be poor, so don't be surprised if you struggle to piece things together.

This diary will help you to make sense of what is happening in your home and will be a useful reference for the future.

PART 1

What Are We Dealing With Here?

CHAPTER 1

What Is Violent Behaviour?

—— Sally ——

Getting our heads around the great big mess of what does and doesn't constitute violence can be fundamental to understanding what is going on in our homes. It can help us peer through the fog and is often the point at which parents and carers start to realize they are living with a great deal more violence than they had initially thought they were. If you have the beginnings of a realization that your house is wallpapered with violence and a cold stone of dread is forming in your stomach, hang on in there. It is a horrible, sad awakening but we are going to guide you through these stages of dread, grief and hopelessness and arm you with the knowledge and skills to untangle the mess.

Defining and describing violence enacted by children, on adults is problematic, to say the least. One of the major difficulties is that we're referring to horrendous behaviour, dished out by children, and more than that, distressed and traumatized children. Perpetrator (bad) versus victim (innocent) is nice and simple. What we're talking about is not simple and it certainly isn't nice.

It would be neat to start with the basic, dictionary definition of violence as an intentional act of physical force, but even that falls over before it gets going. It's that word 'intentional'. Intention, when it is referring to children and violence, is tricky. If acts of violence are intentional, it indicates that a child could stop if they decided to and the nightmare would be over. If it isn't intentional, then should we just accept it, throw in the parenting towel and let the future take care of itself? Neither and both are true, which means we are going to have to step into deeply unfashionable territory – nuance.

As well as nuance, it's also important to understand the scale and frequency of this phenomenon. We are not talking about rare and discrete acts of violence, but multiple acts of physical, verbal and psychological abuse – sustained, dangerous, frightening and undermining. It may become impossible to separate one act out from another and can become a way of life.

What might violence look like in our homes?
The Fireball of Rage
Absolute red-hot raging, thrashing and loss of control is perhaps the most obvious state and source of violence. It is lurching, throwing, punching, smashing, screaming and swearing.

When the Fireball of Rage ignites in your home, or elsewhere, you fear for your life and the lives of others, in a real and terrifying way. There is likely to be damage to property and injury to family members. You may worry that one day someone will get seriously injured, or even killed. Maybe someone already has been injured. You may be frightened for your life in a way that most people never, ever experience. You may lie awake at night worrying that one day you will react, or just do something to keep yourself or someone else safe and end up at the rough end of a police investigation. That's how serious this is.

When others haven't experienced the Fireball of Rage for themselves, they may think it is something of a mega-tantrum. It isn't that. And it doesn't just happen once or twice in a lifetime (although that would be enough) – it may be weekly, daily, or several times a day. The extra crap thing about it is that parents and carers may get to experience their own Fireball of Rage too, when it rips out of us spraying red hot venom. We may not have known of its existence before, but living with violence wakes the sleeping monster inside most of us. They say that violence breeds violence and there is some truth in that. In this context, it's more accurate to say that dysregulation breeds dysregulation.

The where-did-that-come-from?
Some kinds of violence don't send a messenger with a warning; they show up out of nowhere. A sudden slap to the face, or a punch in the

back, is shocking and gives little opportunity to protect oneself. It also makes it extra difficult to work out what set it off and to take measures to prevent it from happening again.

Destruction of property

Pulling doors off hinges, breaking windows and smashing remote controls and screens are some examples of violence directed at property. This may take place during the Fireball of Rage or in what might seem like a cold and calculating manner. It's not accidental damage and it's more complicated than intentional damage, although that's very much how it might come across. There may be certain objects that are targeted, that carry some emotional resonance either for the adult, or the child, or it might be whatever is in reach. As with physical attacks, living among the destruction may become a horrible way of life.

Verbal abuse

Most children reach for mean and offensive words when they are angry and want to cause hurt. What we are referring to as verbal abuse is habitual, extreme and targeted swearing, and violent and threatening language and insults. Insults can include misogynistic, racist, homophobic, size-ist, able-ist and anything else-ist language. The abuse may be muddled and random or will get you where it hurts, in what can appear to be quite a clever and insightful way. Again, we are in the murky waters where intention meets distress and dysregulation. Sometimes dysregulation is nasty.

Intimidation

Intimidation is behaviour that causes fear and alarm and makes a person feel weak, or at least weaker than the intimidator. It can sound like: 'This is what I will do if you don't do what I want', 'Come here and say that', 'Yesterday I bashed someone for doing that', 'I know someone who would sort you out'.

It may manifest itself in body language – a fist getting ready to punch, a flexing jaw, looming up behind, skulking, coming very close, looking menacing, a particular look or a smirk. On their own, these movements, gestures and expressions may not seem like much but as a pattern of behaviour they become abusive. Variations are the subtle shove when you walk past, or the 'You got pranked!' – jumping out to startle you, then laughing like a hyena, or pretending to thump you or flick you in the face 'for a laugh' and finding it amusing when you flinch.

Somewhere down the line, this sort of behaviour merges with controlling behaviour. If a friend told you she was experiencing this at the hands of her partner, you would probably advise her to leave immediately. This scenario can be a good test, if you are ever in any doubt that what you are experiencing is abusive behaviour.

Controlling

Manipulating and manoeuvring others to get a particular need or want met or controlling the emotional temperature in the home and causing distress, disquiet and unhappiness all count as controlling behaviour.

It may be controlling who accesses certain parts of the house, or feeding different information to different members of the household. It could be telling lies about one parent to another, or about a sibling, spreading disinformation and causing fractures in relationships. Or being really pleasant and helpful and then straight away issuing a demand laced with a threat – conditional kindness or charm. It can seem as though it's not enough for the child to get their needs met, they must ensure others in the household are prevented from having theirs met.

It's worth looking at 'gaslighting' as it's a term used to describe a particular type of control and has grown in popularity, particularly to describe abusive control within a couple relationship. In our homes, 'gaslighting', if we choose to call it that, might involve claiming an event or a conversation hasn't taken place, when it has, or has when it never did. For example, insisting that you most definitely agreed they could go to a party or have some money from you, and even describing where you were when you agreed and what you were wearing, and then faking concern or amusement at your bafflement, is gaslighting. 'Don't you remember?' the gaslighter might exclaim, 'You're getting really forgetful!' They may mess about with exact timings and arrangements for things. 'You DEFINITELY said I could stay out until midnight, oh my god I can't believe you're going back on it now.' Little lies, on top of untruths, built on confusion. One thing is for sure, if you call the gaslighter out on their tactics, they will act as though butter wouldn't melt in their mouths. How dare you!

Moving or damaging your belongings could also be classed as gaslighting, if it happens frequently and has a strangeness about it, as could turning down the central heating controls, unlocking the front door at night after everyone has gone to bed and other such mind games that cause you to ask yourself: 'Am I losing my mind?' It's not altogether nice to use terms like this to describe a child's behaviour, but it can be a useful way of clarifying a muddle of confusion and information and to pin this stuff down and talk about it. In order to do that, we can't always couch it in nice words.

When gaslighting is discussed in terms of a couple relationship, the gaslighter is assumed to have full capacity and awareness of their behaviour. They are considered to be clever and manipulative and to be acting in a very cognitive and planned way. We are talking about children and so this is where the comparison veers away.

TIP
Slow things down

If you suspect that your child uses speed and misinformation as a way of getting you to meet their immediate needs, slow things down. 'I'm going to take some time to think about that' is a response that can buy us time to think and prevent us from being bounced into a situation that creates conflict further down the line.

The problem with the term 'domestic violence'

Calling out violence in our homes as domestic violence has some benefits. It can be a useful way to understand our responses to being on the receiving end because it is similar to being a battered and abused partner. The realization can also be empowering and provide some clarity – this state of affairs is unacceptable and cannot continue. But the ultimate measure that an abused partner can take, when they are ready to and have the appropriate support in place, is to leave the relationship. This is not an option open to abused and battered parents. The fact that the 'perpetrators' are dependent children and young people adds a thick layer of complication and nuance.

A word about blaming the child

When talking about violent, controlling and abusive behaviour it is easy to fall into using language that blames the child. It's a defence mechanism when adults are hurting and confused and have a need to vent. The situation is deeply unfair on everyone. There is a place for venting, among peers and with trusted professionals who know that when an adult is expressing something dreadful, they don't really, literally mean it. Venting is important.

Describing the behaviour we live with to those outside the home is fraught with danger. The behaviours are horrendous and there's no other way of putting that. Any person in their right mind would call it out. But the insight and nuance, so often unique to us, is that our child needs help and we need help in order to help them. We have to hold all these complexities, battle with our simplistic good/bad thinking, manage our own dysregulation and dredge up the will to move forward, all at the same time.

A word about blaming parents and carers

Because most people have never shared their lives with distressed children who behave violently, it can all look rather straightforward from the outside looking in. This is especially the case when parents and carers have been so ground down that they present as over-emotional and weepy or inflexible and frozen. It's clearly a discipline problem, you may well be told, so you need to do some or all of the following:

- Put your foot down.
- Put boundaries in place.
- Show him who is boss.
- Switch off the wi-fi.
- Not give her any more money.
- Take away his phone, games console and TV.
- Chuck her out.

You may reach the point where some of these become viable options, but it is way down the line and after everything else has been tried.

For now, they may seem attractively simple solutions and way easier than having to go through the nausea of learning about the art and science of managing violent behaviour and the pain of reconstructing ourselves to be the parents and carers that our children need us to be. There aren't any simple solutions, but that's not to say that there aren't times when we need to employ the simple approach. That's our friend nuance again.

As far as blame goes, no matter how you have arrived at this point, it is not your fault. Everyone who finds themselves in this situation has regrets, for sure, but that's different from taking the blame. Regrets help us to plan how to make improvements. Blame doesn't take us anywhere.

We will go into more detail about why children can behave in these dreadful ways but they are not dreadful children and you are not a dreadful person.

CHAPTER 2

Living with Violence

─── Sally ───

When a storm is forecast, there are three stages – the worry and uncertainty associated with its arrival, the destructiveness of the storm itself and then clearing up the mess it has caused. Violence is similar to a storm, in that it's not just the act that rips up our lives, it's also the expectation of the violence and its aftermath.

Living in fear and dread is torture. It casts a deep, dark shadow and can become such a strong presence that lives become dominated by it and organized around it. A particular time of day, a trigger such as a mealtime or a string of unmeetable demands can all be signs that the thunderclouds are gathering.

The act itself – a punch, push, scream in the face, a prepared fist, smashed-up belongings or whatever it is – may be over and done with in the blink of an eye, or devastatingly drawn out.

It isn't of course over when the act or acts have been carried out. Parents and carers are left emotionally and perhaps physically bruised and can't just dust themselves off and get on with their lives. The bruises last. And the shock lies like a permafrost over homes and hearts. What just happened? How did we get here? And then the anger, outrage, sadness, grief and hopelessness swirl around. There may not be time for these to settle and be processed before the return of the cold dread that another incident is building on the horizon.

Living with violence turns lives upside down and inside out and it impacts on every sphere: relationships, property, finances and health. It tears away at a right to live a fulfilled life in safety, dominates thoughts, derails hopes and plans and erodes individuals. Violence is selfish, demanding, destructive and ugly and it is soul-destroying. When living like this for prolonged periods, parents and carers are no longer the capable, confident, measured people they once were. They become what violence wants them to be, if violence had a persona and an agenda – scared, angry, empty. It's at this point, when parents and carers are at their absolute lowest, that they may be expected to meet services, explain themselves and be assessed.

Blame

Blame is never far from discourses about violence involving children and their parents and carers; looking for someone to blame is a natural impulse after something bad has happened. Blame is easier than deep consideration and humanity for everyone involved. It is also quicker and cheaper and rewards the blamer with a squirt of self-satisfied, self-right-eous smug hormone. The blamee, however, is left feeling worse than ever. 'Not only am I living in hell,' one might reason, 'it is my fault I am here.'

I don't know of a parent who was able to up their game through being made to feel worse than they already did. In order to turn this hideous tanker around, parents and carers have to start by rebuilding themselves, shoring up their foundations and regaining some self-belief. If this is where you are at, we are going to help you to do this. Before we do, it is important to really pin down what violence is and the impact it has.

It feels confusing because it is

Children are not meant to abuse adults. Adults are not meant to be abused by children. All sorts of systems, norms and beliefs are thrown up in the air when this happens. Guilt and innocence, victim and perpetrator – usually such clear and precise concepts – get bent out of shape. Considering violence enacted by children on adults requires sophisticated thinking. And yet there are times when there is value in clarity. It is not acceptable for a child to hit a parent, grandparent, aunt, uncle or carer. If we start to blur the edges, we can get unstuck. It's not even a little bit okay for a child to hit an adult.

We must hold several difficult concepts in our heads at the same time. There may be explanations for the violence, there may be knowledge, approaches and strategies that the adults need to take on board, but it is still a situation that must end, for the good of the adult and the child. It is possible, at the same time, to be compassionate to oneself and towards a child who behaves violently, to help them to change their behaviour, as well as being absolutely firm that violence is unacceptable. It is, however, extremely difficult to hold all these conflicting forces in mind all the time. Because we are human, our approach to complex and brain-aching levels of nuance is to veer off towards one extreme or another.

Cognitive dissonance

Cognitive dissonance is a term that well describes the absolute head scramble that is parenting a child and loving a child who behaves abusively towards you. Cognitive dissonance is when our brain just cannot compute the mental conflicts that it comes up against. It's almost painful for us because we are forced to unpick something fundamental that we thought we knew to be true about the world and which had probably worked well up until this point. It threatens and undermines our grasp of reality. It's a massive deal.

Here are some examples of cognitive dissonance that you may be grappling with:

- 'I love this child and they love me but they hurt me and sometimes I hate them for it.'

- 'My home is meant to be my place of safety and yet I am not safe here.'

- 'I comfort my child after a violent episode during which they have hurt me. I am comforting my abuser.'

- 'If I spot someone who seems as if they might be dangerous, I avoid them. And yet I share my home and life with someone who is a threat to my safety.'

- 'I am the parent or carer and so I am in charge. I set a boundary, such as don't hit me or swear at me, but they cross it anyway. I put in a consequence and it makes no difference, or makes the violence worse. My parenting is making things worse.'

- 'I worry that one day, this child who I love, and who loves me, will kill me.'

- 'I worry that one day, there will be a scuffle, my child will get hurt and tell a teacher that I've abused them. It will be their word against mine. No one will believe me. They will get away with abusing me and I will get into serious trouble for defending myself.'

- 'I am a capable person and yet I don't know what to do.'

- 'This child needs me to be a strong parent or carer for them. This child is doing everything in their power to prevent me from being the strong parent or carer that they need.'

- 'My child needs compassionate and understanding people around them and yet punishes me for being compassionate and understanding.'

- 'My child, who experienced abuse, is now abusing me.'

- 'An hour ago she told me she loves me and now she's telling me she's planning to stab me in my sleep.'

Now can you see why your brain is in pain and why this is an impossibly *difficult* situation to be in?

TIP
Random acts of warmth and kindness

In a violent and aggressive home, warmth and kindness can exit the building leaving us living under a heavy permafrost of resentment. A random act of warmth and kindness is one way to create a spark of hope and love. Examples are putting a sweet somewhere visible for our loved one, giving them a small gift or serving up their favourite meal. If words are possible, keep them to a minimum: 'I thought you might like it' or similar is sufficient. And a word of warning, the giving is entirely unconditional, so don't expect a 'thank you' or even an acknowledgement.

PART 2

Build Knowledge and Skills, Keep Safe and Maintain Boundaries

The traffic light guide for approaching violence

As we take you on this journey to responding to your child's violent behaviour, we are going to think in terms of where we and our children are within our nervous system – our 'states'. We will refer to these states in terms of traffic-light colour zones: Green, Amber and Red.

GREEN represents us when we're safe, calm and collected, fine, happy, working hard, tickety-boo.

AMBER represents us when we are anxious, angry, outraged, hacked off, bent out of shape. From the Amber vantage point, we could either regulate and make our way back towards Green or dysregulate further and head on up into Red.

RED represents us when lids are flipped, horses have bolted, and fans have been hit with shit. We are raging, fuming, aggressive and possibly violent.

Like many tools for managing anger that we use, the traffic

light system is being deployed here too but the reason is quite specific. It is used as an indicator throughout the book to show how we respond to our children when *they* are in each zone but it also helps us to think about where *we* need to be to deploy a certain tool.

CHAPTER 3

Techniques for Avoiding Conflict – The Green Zone

—— **Carly** ——

M ost of the following techniques need to be deployed when every-one is in the Green Zone but some will also be helpful if your child is in the Amber Zone. However, let's be clear about a *very important* point: the vast majority of violence prevention takes place here in the green state.

When you and your child are in the Green Zone, you stand the best chance of avoiding aggression rather than waiting for it to crop up and responding on a whim when everyone's nervous systems are activated for danger. Planning for violence is better than hoping it won't happen.

I have delivered training where aggression and violence in children was one of the key topics. At one of the Q and As, I was asked a lot about children in red, full-blown rage because there seemed to be nothing to calm them, and it was a case of damage limitation. I found myself, again and again, giving advice about Green Zone techniques that would serve to avoid the outburst in the first place or help it not go beyond Amber.

Spoiler alert, there is no magic word or wand once our children are in the Red Zone. It is about surviving and damage limitation in the Red Zone but there's plenty we can do to avoid getting there in the first place...

Here is what the Green Zone looks like:

It's calm. You can smell flowers. Your child is smiling or reading or playing. You are having a chat with a friend without monitoring your every child's move. There is a groove to the flow of your life, and you can, neurologically speaking, multitask. You can put all your energy into silly voices when reading a child their bedtime story. You can appreciate a joke and a laugh. You can discuss politics and ethics. You can plan bits of the future and reflect on the past. If this were a walk in the woods, it would look like you chatting to a friend or relative about future plans, or past experiences while holding hands with your niece and also keeping an eye on the dog. Lovely. You would feel both safe and connected.

It's worth saying that this chapter is about avoiding violence and aggression as opposed to avoiding feelings of conflict. We all experience rejection, disappointment and disagreement in relationships. If you're anything like me, engaging directly with such feelings is far preferable to the festering pustule that is 'passive aggression'. In Western culture, we haven't done a great job creating an environment for interpersonal conflict to be safely expressed. Many of us view conflict as bad rather than progressive and it makes us terribly uncomfortable. So instead of discussing our disconnection, misunderstandings and differing views, we store them all up and they come out in ways that still transmit negativity without being direct about our feelings. And the repression of the words we would use makes the feelings more toxic.

Avoiding anger and aggression in the first place, through operating in the Green Zone, is the quickest way to see improvements. How we do this with easily dysregulated children is a considered approach and can be very different from our usual/learned way of engaging with our children. I have spoken with many parents who have found quick improvements in family atmosphere and increased regulation all round with these techniques because in avoiding the conflict in the first place, regulation leads to regulation.

Safety first

When it comes to safety issues it's a battle we must pick. At no point is it ever going to be okay to be hit, spat at, or have your property destroyed. It's not going to be okay to let your child meet up with a total stranger, deal drugs, kick the dog or bite their sister. We must challenge and try to prevent such things with all our might. That doesn't mean that those things won't happen. Your kids still may engage in those behaviours, but the point is that you have drawn your safety line in the sand and you will do what you can to prevent your child crossing it. You are demonstrating that the thing they want to do or have done is not acceptable or safe.

Testing our value responses

When we become parents, we have hopes, dreams, values, experiences, beliefs, cultural contexts, prejudices that inform our sense of what's okay and what's not. These values hugely shape our responses to our children and the boundaries we create or try to maintain, which means that boundaries are subjective. For example, consider this statement:

I let my 14-year-old child walk home alone from a friend's house at night in the dark.

Please notice your response to that. Now, your reaction to that statement will fall within a pretty large spectrum, ranging from, 'No way, I'd never allow that' to, 'That's absolutely fine'. However you respond will sit within that spectrum and be governed by your values. Keep holding on to your response to that statement. What would happen if I changed the word 'child' to 'daughter'? Does it change your response in any way? I'll do one more:

I let my 14-year-old get their belly button pierced.

What's your reaction to that? Does your reaction change at all if the child's age is 15?

Whether your responses to either of those questions shifted when I changed the parameters or not, I hope you see the point I'm making. We might argue that we live in an area where it's not safe for a 14-year-old to walk home alone. That's based on our experience or knowledge of our area. If we say no to the belly button, that might be because our values say that those piercings are the first step in a slippery slope to something unsavory. Or we might think it's their body, their choice.

When picking your battles, I want to invite you to think about where your values around that issue come from. Experiences (especially those relating to how we were parented), thoughts, prejudices, culture and politics all inform our parenting. Please understand, I am not saying your values are wrong. Or right. I'm inviting you to reflect on why the response you give your child/young person is as it is.

Thinking about this is a great guide in establishing *if* and *how* we apply a boundary because it helps us consider if it's about making *us* feel safe or keeping our child safe. Whether we say yes to walking home at night or no to a belly-button piercing, I think it's right to truly know why it's a yes or no based on our values, hopes and ideals. In my time as a therapist, I have had to invite parents and carers to reflect on why a certain battle they are having over an issue with their child is so important to them. In the process of doing this, parents have found it possible to change their *responses* (not necessarily changed their view or their no to a yes) and take the heat out of the issue.

It takes a lot of guts to examine our values, hopes and ideals because we sometimes discover things about ourselves that we don't like, or it leads us to think about something painful. It is truly a reflection exercise in what really matters, and teasing apart actual safety and emotional safety.

We cannot engage in such a reflection exercise in the middle of conflict but need to do it when we have time and space – when we're in the Green Zone! If you are co-parenting, then this also needs to involve discussing and reflecting with your partner so that you can agree on boundaries. Deciding *if* and *how* you are going to challenge the way your child chows down their food, inhaling it, mouth wide open, is important if eating nicely is a big deal for one of you.

This was something I tried to challenge with one of my kids. It turned out that the value I hold in *actually tasting* food did not align with their need to ingest it quickly, so challenging it caused more negativity in the relationship than it was worth. With another of our children, Mr K's desire for them to be a better, more confident reader manifested in trying to get them to read to him. He placed value on being an efficient reader because that's what our culture tells us is important and that's what we did with our birth children to help them learn to read – why would we not afford this child the same care? Yes, that battle was a source of some fairly volatile interactions and more importantly, relational disconnection. Mr K is a bit ace though, so he thought, 'I'd rather my foster child knows how to read a safe relationship than a book', and he re-evaluated that part of his parental values and adjusted his hopes and ideals accordingly. It was great.

This process is not about allowing everything to go unchallenged. Boundaries make our children feel safe. They convey to our children that we care and sometimes that we are bigger than their fear. I have a great friend called Sarah who experienced multiple abuses as a child and eventually went into care during secondary school. She had several placements. Later she would turn out to be a wonderful support to my family and me while we were fostering. One day we were chatting, and part of the conversation went like this:

Sarah: 'I always knew when a foster placement wasn't going to last.'

Me: 'How?'

Sarah: 'Cos they let me do what I wanted.'

What Sarah went on to say was that the lack of boundaries was a marker for a lack of care.

The 25-year-old principle
Testing our value responses links well to something I call the 25-year-old principle. When parents and carers of teens are being put through the wringer and the very notion of even being a parent to their child is an hour-by-hour battle, I sometimes talk about this principle.

I ask parents to tell me what they would like their relationship to look like when their children are 25. I think I chose this age because it's when our brains are fully developed, we've left adolescence way behind and when we've probably had enough adult life experience to be capable of reflection...but I'm not offering any guarantees here.

So, then parents will say something like, 'I want me and my child to care about each other. I want them to come for Sunday lunch. If they have children, I want to be part of my grandchildren's lives. I want to go for a beer from time to time with them. I want us to hug each other. I want them to be able to talk to me about their lives.' Then I ask them about what decisions and actions they think they need to take *now* to achieve that *then*.

In saying *yes* to granting that night out, I might convey the sense that they have some autonomy and choice and that I am not some evil dictator. If I say *no* to them also staying over at that 'mate's' house afterwards and insist that I pick them up from X at X time, I will maintain their safety and convey that I care enough not to let them go home with someone I don't even know but I suspect is violent or has access to dangerous drugs. Thinking about the 25-year-old principle can be a useful tool to inform, increase and strengthen our capacity to test our value responses.

TIP
Choose your battles

Write a list of all the annoying, unwanted tricky behaviours in your child.

Cross most of it out.

What kind of advice is that?! Well, let me demonstrate. When day-to-day life with our children starts to feel as if every interaction is barbed, it can help to remove a few spikes. Many parents find they have to really examine what they choose to battle over and what they don't. It can be a surprise to many of us how very little really is worth fighting over. In our time parenting children with violent behaviour, Sally and I had to revisit some areas of contention time and again before we realized that it just wasn't worth the fight. When we tell our kids six times to brush their teeth in one morning, everyone gets wound up, not just us. Here's an example showing the battles really worth fighting over:

~~Pull the flush~~

~~Eat using cutlery rather than hands.~~ Maybe only when we're in public

~~Turn lights off~~

Don't hit members of your family/household

~~Don't swear.~~ Maybe don't swear AT me/sister/Dad

~~Hang up your towel~~

~~Go to school on time and with the correct school uniform.~~ (Let school deal with that)

~~Do homework~~

~~Take used crockery out of your room~~

~~Be back home on time.~~ (I still want to aim for this but will settle for my child contacting me to say they'll be late, even if I know they're lying about missing the bus)

Tell me where you are going and with whom (although I know they won't be able to do that when they're in Amber or Red and are leaving the house in those states)

~~Brush your teeth~~

Contrary to popular belief, this isn't an exercise in gross capitulation. It's about us, as parents, taking more charge of the family atmosphere and deciding what really is important in the here-and-now.

Your expectations and list can evolve and change as time goes on but right now, what gives? I'll finish this section with an example.

I don't fully remember all the details, but we were having some sort of gathering for some sort of birthday in some sort of restaurant. It had been a warm day and our foster daughter, Lisa had been out scootering after school for much of the afternoon and was really enjoying herself.

Looking back now, I wonder if this was at a time when her local friendships were forming, and she was desperate to hang out with peers and feared missing out on anything that might strengthen those relationships. I don't truly know, but something about going out that evening to sit still and eat a meal with people she was still learning to read was not a prospect she wanted to engage with over the scootering.

I asked her to brush her hair and get changed. She refused. I'm no stiff-laced Victorian parent but turning up to a meal out in clean clothes and hands felt acceptable to me and I'm not afraid to admit that I was probably somewhat spurred on by how those at the gathering might judge me as a parent if one of my kids came that way.

It went on, me insisting, Lisa refusing. I even called someone very clever and through exasperated breaths asked them why she couldn't do this simple thing. Like I said, I still don't know what was blocking this 'ordinary' precursor to going out for tea for Lisa, but the someone clever invited me to choose between getting to the restaurant just as things were, or me/Mr K staying behind with her.

I came downstairs and announced, 'Come on, let's go out for something nice to eat' because a bedraggled child with us was something I valued way more than a bedraggled child at home feeling that she didn't make the cut for a night out.

Reading their capacity (and our own)

I am not a confident driver. I'm competent and careful but not confident and get no enjoyment from the process.

One day I needed to make a 90-minute car journey to deliver some training, something which at the time, I also found nerve-racking. My preparation was sound. It was before maps were on your phone and I didn't have a sat-nav (for those reading in the future, a satellite navigation device was a device in and of itself that you strapped to your dashboard somehow and it showed you the way). I'd printed out the instructions as to how to reach my destination and left with a full tank of petrol (for those reading in the future, something you used to use to power your car) with plenty of time to spare. It all started well but I hit some serious traffic. Twice. I'd started the journey with a slightly depleted level of emotional and physical capacity because of my anxiety around driving. The first jam depleted me some more. The second jam even more. Here is a diagram of what could have happened to my capacity during this ordeal.

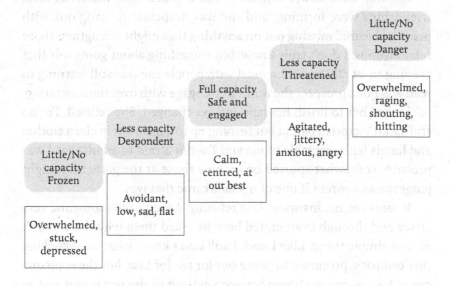

As it turns out, I did feel threatened, sweary and a bit sweaty; however, I pulled over, called the organization to say I might be cutting it fine and found an alternative route to my destination. At some point during the day, I got back to feeling at full capacity, probably at lunchtime. However, if my capacity were stretched even thinner, I might have gone into full blown road-rage with my internal world telling me to get the hell out of there, shouting and swearing at others and banging my fists on the steering wheel. I could also have gone into despondency with my depleted capacity, feeling that I might not make it, bringing to mind other failed journeys or, worse still, have given up altogether and headed home, abandoning the training. I could have been resigned to a stuckness or hopelessness about ever making my destination and avoiding all the calls or emails about it that would follow.

I've used this example to illustrate this idea of our individual capacity to manage any given situation. I'm sure reading this, you can think of situations where you also had enough capacity to see something through or overcome a situation despite it being stressful and your capacity not being at full whack. You can probably think of other times where your capacity was so battered that you were overwhelmed and couldn't carry on. Maybe a physical task like a marathon or an emotional one like screaming at your child when you've tried to be calm with them all day and after they've kicked the dog, bitten their sibling and ignored *everything* you've said all day. What is interesting is that, depending on multiple factors at *any given moment*, the size, amount or bucket-full of capacity we have changes. Here are some examples of what I mean but before you continue, if you are interested in a more scientific break-down of this issue around capacity, please see Appendix A. Go on, it's really cool.

Real-life capacity readings

As you will come to understand, school was a taxing, scary place for our foster daughter Lisa to be. Therefore, during term time, her capacity was somewhat depleted. Usually, during school holidays, it was bolstered and larger. We realized that there were three practical tasks that would assist with Lisa's future and day-to-day life that we could ask of her during school holidays but *not* during term time. These were:

1.   reading signs if she wanted to know about something

2.   walking to the shops to buy one or two things

3.   ordering direct from the waiter what she wanted to eat.

Those might sound small but they weren't. When school holidays came around, Lisa was able to exist with a more sizeable capacity so little 'pushes' of her strengths were possible. In term time, she lived with a greatly diminished capacity and asking her to do any of those three things might result in a swift 'F**K OFF' in your ear drums, or worse, her feeling utter shame because whatever she had guessed was on the menu wasn't actually there.

Let me give you an example from an adult perspective. If you chose to observe me during an 'Insanity' HIIT workout, sweating and straining through some torturous move, and were unwise enough to advise me that I wasn't doing it quite as well as the ridiculously ripped and fit instructor, my response would be to yell 'P*SS OFF!' at you. True story. Twice. There would be two reasons for my outburst.

1.   I am physically under pressure and my breath is an especially precious commodity. I don't have much to spare so what I need to convey must be succinct.

2.   I feel it is something of an arrogant move to offer criticism without being involved.

By all means, offer me support and even constructive critique *if* you are also grubbing around on the floor attempting moving plank walks which you are skilfully manoeuvring *over the dog* who inexplicably always lies in the middle of the front room floor when exercise is taking place. If not, don't. Because of the combination of points 1 and 2, my capacity, both physically and emotionally is depleted, and my response is a tad aggressive. However, I am perfectly capable of relaying my point of view and being shown how to improve in a regulated and reflective way in any other circumstances.

Being able to read where your child is at emotionally enables you to make good judgements about the demands and pressures you put on them at any one time.

Just one more thing about this topic. One of the biggest influencers of capacity when thinking about distressed-based aggression and violence is that due to us as parents/carers usually being the safest people in our children's lives, we are the ones that their brains tell them it's safest to decapacitate with. It's with us that they don't have to hold their breath or grit their teeth or count to ten. Because of this, much of their stored-up anxiety and stress from the day gets processed at home, in their safe space with their safe relationships. It's as if they're saying, 'I'm spent. I just don't have it, and I can't do it'.

Creating YES experiences

1. Have a go!

When we're living with challenging, aggressive behaviours there is a risk that we become, well, risk-averse. We can become entrenched in avoiding *anything* that might trigger an outburst in our child. The difficulty with this is that the trauma limits our breadth of life experiences, which diminishes our capacity for joy, which smashes up our chance for self-care and breeds social isolation. In order to decrease a child's dysregulation, we have to expose them to some level of difficult feelings so we have the opportunity to co-regulate these and, in time, help the child to feel them without going into overwhelm. This isn't about throwing children in at the emotional deep end. It's about sitting with them at the shallow end and splashing your feet about a bit. Creating small, achievable experiences together with your child and quitting while you're ahead is important in increasing their self-worth and ability to tolerate tricky feelings. With planning, you can always deploy an escape route!

2. Say yes to their request

Another slightly different aspect of this is trying to say 'yes' to our children if we can (this has strong links to testing our value responses). When children have early experiences of trauma, they sadly become expectant of negativity in all its forms and are prone to recall present-day negative experiences as opposed to the three hundred lovely things you did for them that day. In fact, even getting a neutral response is perceived as a negative one. These children and young people don't expect to hear 'yes'. So, where you can engineer a yes, it's a chance to discombobulate their survival-based expectations.

3. Lead the way

Perhaps I've made all that sound too easy. The reality is that for you as carers and parents, especially those of us who are single and managing the day-to-day risk of or actual aggression/violence, creating yes experiences can be limited. Maybe the fallout of trying this particular technique has been catastrophic over and over again and you do not have the strength right now to go through it again. If that is you, I wonder if you might be kind and brave enough to give *yourself* the yes experience? Maybe meet with a friend for coffee or go for a walk or watch your favourite film? Is there anything you can do to give yourself a feeling of not being manacled to the manifestation of your child's trauma?

Developmental versus biological age

In the same way that I've encouraged you to read your child's capacity, read their developmental age, not their biological age. Trauma is powerful at interrupting and misdirecting our normal developmental trajectory. In my work with families, we often find ourselves talking with children about how they grew up in a back-to-front or upside down way, first learning how to look after themselves then learning how to be looked after emotionally, physically or both. Perhaps they didn't have time for play because they were so busy watching out for danger, or maybe they couldn't learn to read because they were too hungry and looking out for food. It can be helpful for children to hear this kind of narrative because they often find themselves wondering why they find it hard to do some of the stuff that other kids do with ease which feeds into their own crappy sense of self.

So, while you're in the Green Zone, consider your child's biological age. This will usually be a range, such as two to seven as opposed to a fixed age, depending on how regulated they are in any given moment. Ask yourself what a child that age would be able to do, what they might understand or cope with. I like this because I found that it helped me to hold on to empathy when I was confronted with used sanitary towels smiling up at me from the floor or a red-faced seething toddler in a 13-year-old body. It also helped me make decisions such as:

- Are they ready for a mobile phone?

- Can they go on that sleepover?

- Can they be left at home on their own for an hour?

- How shall I manage pocket money?

Emotional investment currency

Considering an emotional investment currency on items is a helpful strategy which applies to both you and your child. For example, if your child goes in for a bit of property damage when they're raging in the Red Zone, putting away items that you care about might be a good idea.

I let most things go emotionally but I'm still a bit sad about my Wizard-of-Oz-type hourglass and my posh orange wine jug I bought from a lovely artisan market. Equally, if you know that should your child's phone be damaged, Red Zone dysregulation is guaranteed to follow, you may need to negotiate with them that they may only have said phone with the Mega Shock Absorber 3000 (or something with a name like that) protector on it at all times – which they may well take off as soon as you're out of sight!

Using emotional investment currency with your child also opens up a helpful dialogue about their own posses- sions and use of them. Many children/young people have a great deal of difficulty regulating what they say or send in messaging and chat functions on their phone. After losing access to their phones, usually several times for being 'not ready' to use them safely, some young people have been able to hand their phones into their parents in the evenings when much of the 'dissing', 'roasting', sexting and abuse seems to happen. Those young people can place an emotional investment currency on having daytime access to the phone (meaning they're still able to arrange to meet friends and look at social media together during lunch breaks) that is higher than their drive to be involved in messaging during the evenings in unsafe ways.

Do I lock away the knives?

Gosh, if I had a quid for every time someone has asked me that question, I could buy myself something really nice, like a replacement posh orange artisan wine jug.

The truth is that there's no definitive answer to this, but Green Zone reflection is the place from which we make our decision. Practical avoidance measures such as locking away knives, money or expensive items might be called for, particularly if it is a matter of safety. If your child is taking money to buy heroin or threatening to stab you while wielding a knife, I'd say that may well be lock-up o'clock. With items that could potentially be used to harm, my worry about going straight to lock up is that can convey to the child that they are dangerous and reinforce already horribly inaccurate views of themselves being bad, being born bad, being-just-like-their-abusive-parents bad, being-too-dangerous-to live-here bad.

If you are one of those people who have had to lock up items, I'm sorry because it's shit living with a safe in your home. We didn't have to go that far but made a decision to not have any cash lying around or in money boxes. It was just too hard for our girl not to 'make provision' for herself after all those early years of there not being enough – of anything.

Network, network, network

In the years I've been working with families there has been a clear pattern. Generally speaking, those families that have a solid, diverse personal network are better equipped to deal with distress and violence than those without. That's not to say that there is *any* difference in the level of aggression and violence that occurs within family homes; rather, families who have people to support them in different ways have more resilience to deal with the pain and attacks. There are different types of supporters that families need in their networks. Here comes a list – we do *love* a list!

The only-for-you mate

As parents or carers, we need a friend who perhaps doesn't have much to do with our child (the one who is expressing aggression). This friend is the one who takes you out for a pint, coffee, lunch, the latest James Bond film (ohooo, yes please). The two of you may or may not discuss the children but what you will do, ever so importantly, is connect, laugh and have the opportunity to be yourself for a few hours and have a break. Specifically, a break from what a beautiful, compassionate foster carer I had the privilege of working with called, 'relentlessly considered parenting'. This type of parenting is *exactly* what is required of a therapeutic parent/carer and frankly, we *all* need a break from that.

The there-for-my-angry-child mate

Having worked with many children over the years, including aggressive ones, I'm fortunate to be in a position to like almost every child I

work with. And it particularly helps that I don't have to live with them…
(clearly there were a couple of exceptions when I fostered!). You need
someone in your network who understands and loves the bones of your
angry kid and wants to spend time with them, giving them *and* you
respite from one another. I want to be clear, however; beware the adult
who has a sense or, even more dangerously, a claim of understanding
your child above and beyond you…the person who will befriend them
to the extent that they tell you that you've got it all wrong, you've misunderstood your child and they know them better. No, no, no.

The there-for-my-angry-child mate loves you as much as they love
your child and they respect you even more. Their involvement in your
life is for the betterment of your entire family and is founded on compassion and connection. Beware those who found it on fulfilling an
(unknown) unmet need in their own life. It's also important to recognize
that the there-for-my-angry-child mate isn't someone who cannot/
should not challenge them. So often a friend who is connected to our
child is in a better position to challenge them, either playfully or at a
deeper emotional level, because they are not in the role of 'parent' and
have chosen to take an active involvement in our child's life. They don't
have to be there, but they are. They can be well placed to talk about the
choices a child or young person is making without inducing shame.

The there-for-my-angry-child's-sibling mate

You obviously know where I'm going with this. It absolutely doesn't
matter whether the other siblings who are also living with aggression/
violence are birth children, other foster children, other adoptive children, whatever. In the same way that your angry child needs a someone
who gives them unconditional positive regard, if you have another
child or children, they also need someone who will look out for them,
hang out with them and give them a joyous or chilled break from the
difficulties at home. Again, they cannot be someone who bad-mouths
the angry child, but who can sensitively accept and contain whatever
ranting, crying or swearing that child might need to do. These mates
can be a little sanctuary for siblings without making them feel as if they
understand them, but you (the parents/carers) don't. I'm guessing you're
starting to see a theme here?!

The I'm-totally-up-for-learning mate

These might be quite surprising and not necessarily mates, but people in your personal or professional network who notice that you, as a family, are part of something difficult, complicated and needing compassion. You arouse their curiosity, and they jump on the rickety, swervy train that is your family journey. Several of our lovely mates fell into this and other categories. To be honest, I wasn't surprised because they were already awesome people who would do that kind of thing. But there are sometimes people who surprise us. For us, it was a brilliant teacher, whom I will call Mr A. He recalls going 'head-to-head' with our foster daughter and 'losing' as she walked off the playing field while yelling at him that he was a 'f**king goon'. After that point, he went out of his way to learn all he could about our kid and liaised with us on almost a daily basis in an attempt to create the safest environment in school as was possible for her as well as keeping the dialogue going about where she was at emotionally in the wider context. He was a godsend.

The utter-gold-dust mate

This mate does a bit of everything. I was massively blessed with two or three of these, one of whom was Sarah, who I mentioned earlier. They love you, your partner, *all* your kids. They are forgiving when your child hurts theirs or steals their money. They take your other kids out for pizza or keep them in for lunch in front of *The Tweenies* when the social workers come over or when you have to deliver a firm 'no' (see Chapter 7). You can call them at 3am in the morning and they'll meet you across the road in PJs with a roll-up. They don't even mind when your blubbering snot lands on their shoulder. Talk about doing someone a solid.

Due to the way which living with violence affects us, it may be that those in your network genuinely have no idea what you are going through or what you need. You may need to be a bit vulnerable and make the first move, such as telling a friend how tough life is and how much you could do with someone else putting your child to bed one night per week. Or how much you need them to go for a coffee with you and just listen or not expect you to talk about home life at all. You may need to take risks, allowing that family member to have them overnight, knowing your child will be spoilt and pumped full of sugar and horrible to you the following day but at least you get a break and can, of course, develop a narrative around how 'That's okay at Auntie Sophie's house because she's your auntie and it's her job to spoil you but at home with me, I have to stick to the boring rules because that's my job as a safe daddy... it's what safe daddies do!'

Summary

- Read where your child is at. Can they manage the demand or situation they are being faced with?

- Trauma is predictable and we can use this to reduce control potency and better prepare our children for situations.

- Try to say yes – it might not be so bad. And even if it is, you've learned something.

- Consider how old your child is emotionally and whether they will manage or be ready for the potential situation or item they wish to acquire.

- Put away or hide items that you value that your child could throw, steal or ruin.

- If you are sure they might use an item as a weapon, lock it away.

- Your number one asset is your network. Always.

CHAPTER 4

The Biology of Trauma

—— Carly ——

There are biological reasons why children become aggressive (and adults, for that matter). The children and young people we are thinking about flip out, lose their cool, get stuck, oppositional and immovable. It's useful to know a bit about the biology behind this because it helps to make sense of the resultant behaviours and develop strategies that work *with* our biology and not *against* it. Understanding the biological reasons why aggressive or violent behaviours occur helps us to:

- have empathy

- parent with and not against their and our biology

- let go of strategies that don't work.

I'm going to take you through the basics of this stuff with enough detail to inform your parenting but as with when we looked at the issue of capacity above, there'll be additional, more scientific material in the Appendices. If you find the rest of this chapter helpful, I'd advise you to take a look. I'm going to introduce some mega-helpful concepts that I have used, not just in informing my therapy practice or my care of children but also in helping those children to understand themselves. In turn, this lessens how responsible, weird and scary they feel about themselves, which for me is the best bit about all of this.

Anger isn't all bad

Anger is okay. Like, really okay. Righteous anger changes things that need changing. Or it upholds something that needs upholding.

So many times, I have given children permission to be angry about their early lives. The abuse, the injustice, the suffering they endured was *not okay* and never will be on any level. It's fine to be angry about that. It is acceptable to be angry if someone damages your car and drives away or angry with yourself for losing your ring. Anger is a human emotion and it's there for good reason. This is important because I think many children believe (or maybe get the message?) that being angry is not okay and only 'bad' children feel anger. Of course, that is a total crock, but it feels part of our culture.

My role as a foster carer or a therapist is not to 'get rid' of anger in children. It's to understand it and sometimes normalize it and help children feel it without becoming violent. And even then, there are children I have worked with who move from a place of hurting others when they're angry or smashing up rooms to yelling 'F**k!' and slamming a door and that is acceptable in their family as an expression of their anger.

There are things I am angry about and I'm glad I am angry about them. When thinking about anger, I want to get to the heart of what children and young people can/should be angry about rather than trying to erase that emotion.

Attachment

When a human baby is born, they are completely and wholly dependent on their carers for survival and as a result, make their needs known by crying/sleeping/grimacing/arching their back. That's not really a sophisticated repertoire of capability, is it? But it is absolutely vital to their survival and it follows that all the other skills and behaviours they learn are too, such as smiling, crawling, feeding themselves, sitting up, lifting their heads, pointing, walking (to something or away from it), talking, whining, washing, wiping, learning to write and read, do a bit of maths, tell a joke or understand one, make friends, learn from mistakes, take the correct dose of paracetamol and avoid eye contact in a lift (elevator for our American readers) at all costs.

Babies are utterly dependent on us for their every need to be met for a long time, certainly longer than other mammals. As parents, we must provide them with all their basic needs and read which one of those has to be met, for quite some time. If they are met with relatively consistent, responsive caregiving, over time the child will develop certain expectations about themselves and their world. For instance, the desperate cries of a hungry new-born baby become less desperate after three months if they have learned to expect to be fed in a timely manner from when that hunger starts. In meeting their basic, physical needs in this way, we also develop their emotional needs. To be clear, that's not about meeting needs basically, it's about meeting basic needs in a considered, baby-centred, warm, curious, often playful way, even when it's hard to do that at 3am. How we, as caregivers, meet a child's needs is important because they learn about themselves, relationships and the world from us. Specifically, they learn whether:

- they are loveable and worthy or bad and worthless

- that adults meet their needs or that adults sometimes meet their needs or that adults don't meet their needs or that adults are dangerous and frightening

- that the world is an interesting place to explore or that the world is unpredictable or scary.

The way we respond to a child's needs is therefore hugely influential and, generally speaking, the window for them forming this inner guidance system about themselves, relationships and the world – something that's called their *internal working model* – is between pre-birth and three years old.

Attachment styles
There are four basic types of attachment style that develop out of the care they receive, though it's not unusual for a person to have a mixture of styles.

Secure attachment: This is formed where the child expects relationships to be mostly reliable, reciprocal, loving and playful. Emphasis on the word *mostly* because perfection is not required. They feel able to seek out key attachment figures to have their needs met, for example when they need a snack or are scared or when they fall over and hurt their knee or when a stranger talks to them. They learn to explore the world through the safe base of their attachment figures and when anything goes wrong, either they can increase their proximity to that caregiver or the caregiver will go to them with regulatory messages about whatever has upset or bothered their little one.

Insecure-avoidant attachment: This is formed where the child mostly expects relationships to be one-sided, with others seeking to put their own needs first. These children rely on themselves to get their own needs met so don't try to seek help when they fall over, minimizing their felt needs. They will mainly ignore strangers and will go headlong into the environment, scanning and checking and assessing for danger all by themselves. They always stride ahead of their parents/carers into my therapy room and pick up anything they see of interest without any sense that asking for it is required.

Insecure-ambivalent attachment: This is formed where the child has no sense of whether their need will be met or not and the main feature of the parenting style associated with this is oscillating inconsistency between the child being neglected or ignored to being very important in terms of getting the carer's own needs met. Children with this style of attachment fear being unseen so maximize their needs and can be clinging and attention-needing but also don't have a clear sense of how to utilize the regulation, care and comfort you are trying to give them. Being in a relationship with someone very organized in this way can feel like a game of 'I hate you, don't leave me' and 'I love you, back off'.

Disorganized attachment: This is formed where the child's experience of caregiving is frightening, highly neglectful, abusive or repeatedly abandoning. Due to such overwhelming experiences coming at them from all sides, their only 'style stratagem' is control and their organizing feeling is fear. There is no one or group of behaviours that is neatly descriptive of how their attachment style looks but if you are in a relationship with them, you feel it intensely. They are highly mistrustful and full of shame (see later in this chapter). They may be highly compliant and charming or highly oppositional and physically destructive.

Of course, it is more nuanced than clearly delineated attachment styles and people often can hold a 'mix' of attachment styles. For example, I'm mostly secure with a decent dollop of avoidance. It helps me to be aware of that so I can try to avoid avoidance where it becomes unhelpful. I've known children who have a disorganized attachment style but the safer they feel and more regulated they become, they operate more out of an ambivalent or avoidant pattern.

This next point about attachment styles is very important. I have used some powerful descriptors about children, their feelings and their behaviours but these are children who grow to be adults who are worthy of love and care irrespective of how they feel about themselves. They are brave, savvy, intelligent, funny, helpful, kind, creative, innovative, sparky, plucky, loveable and bloody brilliant. They also have capacity for change like all humans and although attachment is powerful, it is not endlessly deterministic but nuanced and influenced by many relationships and life experiences. Difficult experiences of any kind in life, particularly those that are ongoing, can be tempered (excuse the pun) by a loving Granny, an encouraging teacher, an invested employer, a best friend, an unexpectedly kind and patient partner, even a child. Or circumstantially, a football scout sending you in a progressive direction, a steady or creative or interesting job like you've never had before, or joining a band. It's usually the interpersonal relational stuff that really makes a positive difference.

At the heart of why attachment is central to our sense of safety are two things. First, there is a *biological* basis for attachment behaviours and our responses to danger, and second, *trust* and *emotional regulation* don't even develop when attachment experiences are poor.

Activated attachment isn't always what it's cracked up to be

When I work with families for whom aggression and violence is an expression of distress, there is often a discord between the parents and their personal and professional support network. This centres around the fact that, in most cases, violence occurs at home. Parents are usually the target. It doesn't happen with the social worker, or in residential, or with Auntie Maude. The network starts to wonder what it is that parents are getting wrong to elicit such extreme responses from their child. Now the dynamics and complexities of this will be explored more fully in later chapters and I wouldn't do therapy the way I do if I didn't believe that parents and their parenting approach can be the main agent of therapeutic change in children. However, I think a large part of the reason why violence only happens in the family home isn't because of poor parenting – it's because the parental relationship, *the very act of being a parent to a child*, activates their attachment system. When children, for whatever reason, have aggression and violence as part of their attachment behaviour repertoire, it gets played out with those who trigger (in positive and negative ways) their attachment system. As Brene Brown[1] points out, attachment is not the same as love. Attachment *is* conditional – 'Meet my needs!' It cries.

Nervous states and sensing

I'd like to start this section by slowing things down and asking you how you are feeling right now:

- Are you calm?

- Are you addled because you're trying to read this but keep getting interrupted?

- Are you low or sad?

- Are you numb?

- Have you come to this section furious about something I've written or some incident that prompted you to pick this book up?

- Are you anxious or curious?

Now I'd like to ask you what you are sensing right now:

- Are you warm or cold or just right?

- Can you feel your duvet over your legs or your bottom against the chair or your elbows on the table?

- Can you hear birds?

- Can you hear the sea? (If so, I envy you.)

- Are you clammy or feeling fresh?

- Do you sense pain in your body?

- Are you tired or energized?

- Can you smell anything or taste your toothpaste or coffee or something more exciting?

How we FEEL + what we SENSE = our STATE

What's strange and a bit sad about distressed violence in children is that the behaviour is *actually* them trying to get from a sense of *unsafe state* to sense of *safe state*.

It's important to recognize that our nervous system and brain are an addition to the better-known senses of taste, touch, smell, sight and hearing. They are an unseen but highly powerful sense that works in all kinds of ways with other senses. One of their key functions is to sense safety and unsafety. If they sense safety, then they carry on as they were. If they sense unsafety, they tell the body to jolly well do something about it FAST, and which kind of unsafety it detects depends on how our bodies respond to get us back to safety. Here's how it works:

STATE	LIFE THREAT	SAFE	THREAT	DANGER
Action	Freeze: stuckness, numbness, hiding, high avoidance	Social, calm, engaged, at your best	Flight: alert or alarmed, walking or running away	Fight: shouting, screaming, punching, destructive

Let's say you're in a state of safety while catching up with a friend at a coffee shop.

You hear a loud crash from somewhere nearby. In that moment, your smile disappears, your face becomes flat, and your eyes widen and turn towards the noise. You have moved into a state of threat. Within a second or less you realize that the noise is the sound of something that has fallen and there is no danger. You return to eye contact and coffee. But you were in a state of threat; your body was checking whether the crash meant danger. In fact, it was going through the entire back catalogue of every experience you have had with loud crashes and scanning them for information about whether that kind of crash is safe or not. If your brain has filed crockery-crashes in the safe file, you'll return to a state of safety.

Maybe your eyes will also help you make that call but usually the brain gets there first. Now imagine that you had, in the past, an experience or experiences that your brain/nervous system remembered as threat or danger. What might happen under those circumstances is that you might dive under the coffee shop table, or scream or lash out at your unwitting friend, all of which would render difficult consequences for which you had little or no control. These behaviours are undesirable, unwanted and considered *bad*. That's what happens for many of the children we are considering in this book. This is not an easy situation, and it makes getting back to a state of safety more tricky because you're then filled with shame (again, see below).

Thinking about states helps us to understand where we or our children are in our nervous systems. How our body needs to interact with the world depends on how safe we perceive it to be in any given moment. It is also noteworthy, if not essential, that we recognize the order of *flight* then *fight*. Now, if you're thinking, 'I know/live with children who just do fight' then bear with me. When we perceive danger, our bodies mobilize; they get ready for action. We try to run first but if that fails, we then move to fight. However, if our story so far has presented our nervous system with evidence that there is nowhere to run or that running doesn't work, we will pass straight through this stage further towards *fight*. This is where we're at if we become violent...thinking brain diminished, action brain pumped.

Like me, you may have also experienced your child(ren) in freeze, when demobilization or shut-down is the result of perceiving life threat. Again, a person may go through flight and fight but pass into freeze when these fail. Or just like the short-cut to fight, life may have taught them that the best response to sensing danger or life threat is to head straight to freeze. We return to a safe state when the body perceives that life threat or danger has passed, but many children, young people and adults live their day-to-day lives perceiving threat/danger all over the place so their bodies are wired for action at any given moment and are therefore more easily triggered into aggression or violence. Appendix B gives more detail about this.

Triggers and tolerance

I'd like to link this section to capacity that I mentioned in Chapter 3. I want to use this to think about triggers and dysregulation. If your child gets sent into fight mode, it's because the danger they are sensing has pushed them beyond their capacity. But the size/amount/bucket-full of our capacity isn't static. It can change day to day or minute to minute and is influenced by a multitude of factors within us and our environment. Imagine the following fictional scenario:

It's Monday morning and seven-year-old Josie is in foster care. She is in foster care because of serious neglect and exposure to domestic and substance abuse. At the weekend, her birth parent didn't show up for the monthly contact they have, and she doesn't know why. Josie finds school difficult and the first part of today is maths – her least favourite subject and one she is way behind her peers with. She manages to get through maths and it's breaktime. She plays with her best friend outside and when they come back in for snack time, the only fruit left is a banana, which she absolutely hates. The rest of the morning goes well although by lunchtime she is very hungry. She runs to get to the front of the lunch queue and is told off for doing so and sent to the back of the line. She eventually gets to eat her food, which she wolfs down to get outside to play before her friend starts playing with someone else. In the afternoon, there is a supply teacher as her own teacher has gone on some training. Josie is very quiet because she doesn't know this teacher and the topic is 'families'. Josie gets told off for fidgeting and later the teacher picks her out to share with the class something about her family. Josie remains silent and so the teacher asks her again. When Josie remains quiet, another child volunteers out loud, 'She hasn't got a mummy'. Josie leaps from her chair, screams an obscenity at the child then flees the classroom, knocking over pencil boxes, books and display work as she leaves.

Did you spot the triggers? They weren't difficult to see from here but if that were a real-life situation, many of those triggers would have been hard to identify, including for poor Josie. And how is the foster carer, whose job it is to regulate this child and help her with her feelings, supposed to know about all these triggers? With each trigger, Josie's capacity becomes thinner and thinner and what with it being Monday and her not getting to see her birth parent that weekend, it isn't as if she had much capacity to start with. Exposure to triggers and the size of our capacity are key factors in this violence discussion because identifying and reducing the first while identifying and increasing the second is crucial in our approach to managing violence, both in terms of avoiding it and in terms of the repair. You could put what I just said into a formula:

$$\text{Decreased triggers} + \text{Increased capacity} = \text{Regulation}$$

Let's look at some examples of what can make us sense unsafety.

I like parties. I like music, dancing, chatting and other stuff that makes a gathering a party. When I was a kid, I was at a New Year's Eve party with members of my family. I was having a lovely time until midnight. At midnight hundreds of balloons were released from a net high above our heads in the hall we had been having fun in. I froze, then I put my hands over my ears and ran from the room into the reception area. I went from feeling safe to feeling afraid in a perfectly safe environment – an environment where everyone else was having fun.

I fear inflated balloons. Yes, I just said that, and I mean it. My brain sensed danger when those balloons fell because it scanned all my experiences before that moment and decided that based on that, balloons were unsafe. I remember a big balloon bursting right in my face when I was small and it was a shock and it hurt, and it definitely played a part in balloons going into the *not safe* section of my brain…maybe other experiences also contributed to that, but I don't remember those. Whatever the reason, my body senses that balloons are not safe and they are, therefore, a trigger.

In addition to attachment, internal working models, capacity and triggers, let's think about kinds of stuff that affects our personal constitutions of safety and unsafety. I hope some of these will ring a bell or two about the children you are thinking about or even for yourself.

Safety and unsafety
Developmental trauma
We all experience stress. We are meant to, in short bursts, to help us do our best or manage what is difficult. That test, that interview, that first date. Stress gets shit done, psychologically, educationally and practically. As babies and toddlers, the way we are supposed to develop and grow

is to have our stress regulated for us. Not *removed*, but *regulated*. Not *placated*, but *soothed*. Across the lifespan, stress is supposed to enhance our lives one way or another.

Developmental trauma (also called complex trauma) refers to prolonged episodes of *relational* traumatic stress, particularly in pre-birth or early childhood and because, as previously explored, we are utterly dependent on our caregivers for every aspect of our survival during those years. The sources of developmental trauma are varied. They include premature birth with the long hospitalization and intrusive procedures that go with it, or no prematurity but any reason for long/ multiple periods of hospitalization and intrusive procedures. It could involve substance misuse in-utero or maternal stress of any kind such as being a victim of domestic violence or, like me, someone you care a great deal about goes missing and is subsequently found having committed suicide and then there is the pain and confusion and funeral-going that follows such a tragedy. The equivalent in adults is post-traumatic stress disorder, when adults exposed to chronic, unregulated stress begin to live safely but they are invaded by thoughts, feelings, flashbacks, nightmares, pathologies and somatic (bodily) reactions that convey a belief that danger remains live and present.

A baby can experience *stress* but if their stress is not regulated by a parent, it becomes *unregulated stress* which, if it happens regularly, is *traumatic stress*. This includes in-utero stress that the pregnant female experiences and is passed through the placenta (because hormones are weeny enough to make those tiny gaps) into the developing baby. Anything that keeps a young child in repeated and prolonged states of traumatic stress forces the child to survive their environment in any way they can and to be highly biased to perceiving danger and life threat within their environment years after they begin to experience actual safety.

(Unmet need = unregulated stress) x A large number = Traumatic stress and developmental trauma

With developmental trauma, our brains develop actual neural connections and pathways that are conditioned for a world of unsafety. Developmental trauma is *relational* trauma...and it gets played out relationally for better or for worse, in joy and in fear. Children with developmental trauma are likely to have disorganized attachment styles (see above) and are easily triggered into states of threat, danger and life threat. In fact, some children spend more times in these states than they do in states of safety. They need therapeutic parenting in order to feel safer and more regulated.

Shame

This small word is directly behind the vast majority of any episode of violence and aggression in children and young people. Shame is what we feel when something goes wrong but we are unable to attribute the 'wrong' to circumstance or choice. We can only feel the wrong in terms of us being the wrong or the bad. How does that happen? When we are toddlers we experience the world with a new sense of autonomy, expectancy and bravery that we do not have in our babyhood. We walk towards objects or toys, we reach out for them, we make adults or other children laugh and our egos are on top form. But when, mid-ego-tastic adventure, we are abruptly stopped in our tracks or something doesn't happen the way we were expecting, it results in this emotional crash.

For example, let's imagine a toddler who is taken to a new environment. There are toys and interesting stuff to look at, touch and put into your mouth. Your parent gets momentarily distracted talking to another adult while you notice a big orange wobbly thing at the end of the room. It sparks your interest, and you begin to utilize your new-found walking skills to go towards it. As you get close you reach out your hand towards it, intending to touch it. Then all of a sudden you hear 'NO!' being shrilled at you. You are shocked and stop immediately, and then a feeling quickly follows. That feeling is shame. It's big and ugly and overwhelming. It causes you to look down towards the floor – you might stay like that or cry. Hopefully what happens next is you hear your parent's voice again but this time it carries some urgency, but one that is soft and absolutely wants to convey safety. It probably says something like, 'Oh my goodness, it's okay! I didn't mean to shout; it's just that the fire is so hot and you could hurt yourself!' At the same time, the parent will usually have also increased their proximity to you, picked you up and held you close while they put meaning and words to what on earth you have just experienced. You might not understand their words or have a clear sense of what just happened, but you will be having your shame regulated. When we are little, as multiple episodes of shame are regulated, our shame becomes guilt. Shame is a mechanism for socialization. But if our shame is not regulated because our 'regulators' are absent, or they are the *source* of our shame or tell us to stop snivelling, then it remains as shame. The problem with that is when something goes wrong, we come to believe that we are the source of the problem – that we are the bad, the junk and the wrong. Guilt says 'I did a bad thing'. Shame says 'I am bad'. Unregulated shame becomes 'pervasive shame';[2] the strength and depth of it is all consuming and when it comes to violence, it's like rocket fuel for igniting it.

Let me give you a couple of examples.

Lisa loved her scooter. One day, after church, she scooted off towards home. I walked behind her. Fifty metres ahead, she tripped and fell off the scooter. There were several people around her who approached her to see if she was okay. She was curled up in a ball, head down, unable to respond to anyone. That was the shame. As I got close, I thanked the people who were around and told them that she was fine. Lisa didn't move. Once they had dispersed, I got down on the pavement next to her, put my hand on her back and said, 'It's okay, they've all gone now. You can have a hug if you need one'. I understood the minute that she came off her scooter that she would be in shame and unable to manage the 'audience'. I got people away from her as soon as I could because their presence might trigger aggression if she felt exposure on top of the shame. My telling her that the coast was clear, and she was safe to connect, regulated that situation.

A classroom of children has just been given their spelling test results. There is a reward system whereby children who get full marks make a tally next to their name on a visual leader board. There are rewards at the end of each term for kids with one set of full marks or more. One lad, James, for whom spelling is not his strong subject on account of undetected dyslexia, never gets to put a tally by his name. After several terms of getting 2, 3 or 4 out of 10, this lad decides to put a tally by his name when he thinks the teacher isn't looking. Another pupil sees him do it and is surprised given that everyone knows he is bad at spelling. The boy questions James and James insists he got full marks. The other lad then turns and yells towards the teacher, 'Miss, did James get 10 out of 10?' James goes into toxic shame at being exposed when he already feels like crap about his spelling ability and lashes out, pushing the other lad to the floor. James is sent to the headteacher's office for a reprimand.

Individual events/experiences

The following list is not exhaustive but each of these warrants their own recognition. They all follow the same principle of my experience with the balloon but have their own unique flavour.

Bullying

I have met a sad number of young people with significant anxiety difficulties who could trace the source of that anxiety to being bullied. Being bullied essentially results in you, as the victim, feeling small, vulnerable, sad, afraid and worthless. We risk believing the lies that bullies tell us. It can lead to self-loathing and self-harm. Going into school or on to a social media/messaging app on a phone (those are where most bullying occurs) can be *very* unsafe and traumatic when bullying is what welcomes you.

Death

I don't know about you but when I hear about the death of anyone I have been loosely connected to or someone connected to a friend, I get really sad and cry. That is a very normal reaction for many people. But I wasn't always that way. Don't get me wrong, I wasn't what my mate would call 'dead inside', far from it. But once I had lost a couple of people, particularly my Granny, I started to feel the pain of losing someone to death much more acutely. This might seem a strange example to give since death isn't 'safe' as such. The point I'm trying to make is that the pain that I felt when I lost someone gets recalled and replayed emotionally whenever I hear of others' losses. Therefore, there is sometimes something about the nature of death that rears its head repeatedly and contributes to our sense of unsafety. The same is true for when we suddenly lose someone from our lives in other ways, such as moving cities and losing best friends or familiar surroundings. With people who just 'up and leave' when we never expected them to, like family members serving in wars, even if they come home five years later, their departure is sudden and uncertain in outcome.

Displacement

This covers rather a number of experiences. I'll start with one many of us have experienced: the arrival of a sibling. For some of us this will have occurred resulting in the most minor of reactions – a tilt of the head, a frown, a bit of an inconvenience. For others, it might be a little more like one of my best friends who, aged seven, asked his mother, 'Can we throw the baby in the bin now?' But neither of these reactions will mean that our brains will regard the arrival as unsafe. For others, it is much more significant. Perhaps being the apple of a parent's eye, their whole world, then suddenly finding themselves having to move over for a human they never thought would exist. Or perhaps that new baby/child is very ill, needy, demanding and requires a huge level of attention from parents that was previously bestowed entirely on them? It could start even earlier than this. For children who grow and develop in a womb surrounded by smell and sounds from one mother, one family, one culture only to be born and handed over to a different family, a different culture. Or fast forward to slightly later in life. Something my professional experience has taught me is that when we are born and raised in a family, irrespective of what kind of family that is, we never, ever imagine or contemplate being removed from that family or losing them. The second that actually happens, we always wonder when it might happen again. If we are displaced from the family we know, we will fear displacement again at some level in our psyche. For children who lose their homes and their homelands to war, oppression and other evils, how can we expect their nervous systems to respond other than with abject fear and uncertainty?

Divorce

Parents can separate well or not, and all variations in the middle. On one end of the spectrum, we have folk who, post separation, are more amicable than they were when together and they keep their children's emotional health a priority. At the other end of the spectrum is that awful car crash of a split where the adults hate each other, and the children feel it all. When we are thinking about safety, I don't want to dwell on where on that spectrum is traumatic and where it isn't. It's much more about the extent to which a child internalizes a sense of responsibility (for the split), a sense of loss and a sense of anger. What a child thought was their world, is not. It is like displacement in many ways. Because of their attachment systems, children are geared up to have a sense of how their attachment figures are doing: happy, sad, busy, distracted, irritable, and so forth. When divorce and separation occur, significant emotions will inevitably be present for parents, some of which may be new to their child's experience, and they will pick up on these to greater or lesser extents. Even when divorce/separation comes as a 'relief' for all involved, children can still be left with complex issues around loyalty or which parent needs them the most or how they are going to explain it to their best friends. When separation happens, children can feel a complete disintegration of any control or predictability in their lives. That is scary, and fear is the most common trigger for aggression and violence.

Discrimination

This issue ranges from subtle to blatant, from unknown to intentional, for a short period of our lives to the whole lifetime. When we live our lives against a backdrop of discrimination, whatever form it takes, we are placed in the position of other. Lesser other. Less worthy, less entitled, less valued. At its worst, discrimination de-humanizes. Whether it is our gender, the colour of our skin, our race, sexuality, ability status, economic/class status, gender or family status (specifically those children and young people who do not grow up in their family of origin), discrimination sends a message about us, about aspects of us that we are, not what we choose. Sadly, that message is not a good one. If we are surrounded by discrimination as we grow up, is it at all a wonder that our nervous systems develop the need to fight? If we experience a one-off traumatic experience of discrimination, especially one we were not expecting that turns our sense of safety on its head, does it not make biological sense to be more on our guard and that we are forced into a space where we grieve and need to re-evaluate our safety, grasping onto any form of control possible?

Discovery

This is about discovering something about your world that undermines it. It tells you what you thought you/your world is, is not, so it puts your identity in question. That makes you confused, which *can* make you feel shame...and so on.

Illness, hospitalization and pandemics

There will be many of us reading this who have experienced the necessarily (sometimes life-saving) intrusion of a hospital check-up. For those living with a condition that requires medical monitoring or intervention, life is rather organized by it. Sometimes that treatment or those drugs or that scan or that injection can feel like a violation. If you are too young to understand what is happening and why, it can be a terrifying experience to be held and touched and poked and prodded by strangers. For babies born prematurely or needing immediate surgery, the sense of coming into a dangerous, strange, loud, bright, bleeping and beeping world must be overwhelming. I remember when some of our best friends gave birth to their son at 27 weeks and I went in to hospital to see him. Jayden was tiny, clearly not fully formed with translucent skin and wires held onto his body with tape. He was in a Perspex box and was covered in bruises from heel pricks and cannulas. We could only hold his hand through a hole in the box. The level of monitoring was huge, and all those machines must have sounded so loud to his tiny, not-yet-ready ears. He would have had a sense of what his pain and fear was and none of us could tell him. Illness and hospitalization might involve being physically separated from your parent when you need them the most. It might be because whatever your condition or injury, pain is involved, especially recurring pain. When there is a question mark over whether you are going to die or not, it certainly is *not* safe...

And that's just them. For children who love and live with that person, there can be a significant impact on them too. The sibling whose own life gets organized by their poorly brother or sister. For the child whose Mummy or Daddy is injured or has cancer or any other condition that means that for them, the most important person in their world is not okay. Witnessing others' pain can be intensely more traumatic than bearing our own.

And I really don't want to talk about it but I have to. The events following the pandemic of 2020 have taught us all that living through such events is traumatic. A state of international emergency resulted in collective fear, anger, anxiety, loss and uncertainty. Some of my nieces and nephews spent a half, third and quarter of their lives in lockdown, deprived of the regular socialization experiences that we had at their age. Many of us feared for the lives of our parents or grandparents or were keyworkers exposed to coronavirus on a daily basis. Simply being unable to see our friends and loved ones, the people who make us feel human and connected, was traumatic. Equally traumatic was the unknown. We did not know how long lockdowns would go on for, what would happen or when the effects and consequences of the virus would end...

Even when vaccines arrived, there was and continues to be uncertainty about side effects and government motives. We argued among one another about it. Countless holidays, weddings, bar/bat mitzvahs, football games and funerals have been rearranged, cancelled or reduced to a few attendees, unable to hug or sing or dance. Our capacity for joy was seriously compromised and our ability to emotionally withstand those disappointments wore thinner and thinner. Was it traumatizing? Bloody right it was.

Summary

Given that this chapter was a tad hefty, here is a summary of what we covered.

- We and our *attachment styles* are shaped by our experiences and designed to adapt to the care we receive and the environment we find ourselves in.

- Our bodies are constantly scanning the environment for change, and we sense safety or danger.

- When our bodies *sense* danger, we go into states of *flight, fight* or *freeze* before we become safe again.

- Aggression and violence occur when we are in a *state of fight*. We go through flight before fight.

- Our *capacity* to manage any given physical or emotional situation is changeable and depends on a multitude of internal and external factors.

- We develop/learn *triggers* throughout life that associate certain experiences with threat and danger. These triggers are not necessarily unsafe; we just associate them with danger.

- Babies and toddlers who experience unregulated, toxic stress over time may experience developmental trauma. Such children are easily triggered into states of flight, fight and freeze.

- There are many kinds of life experiences that can create triggers for our bodies to sense unsafety.

CHAPTER 5

When Things Begin to Escalate – The Amber Zone

—— Carly ——

Welcome to Amber Zone aggression. That sounds like a featured area in the TV show *The Crystal Maze* but sadly it is not. It's much more difficult. It might be helpful to go back to the idea of *states* for a minute.

Our nervous system does not clunk between states such that we can only be fully out of one to be wholly in the next. It's not a switch, but is lengths and lengths of neurons. It's more of a flow, even for those of us who have been on the end of an explosive outburst when seconds prior we felt as though all was complete calm. To that end, we can take advantage of those states that are definitely not at the safest end of safe and social but not in the thick of fight – the in-between bits. This is where this chapter is set.

Here is what Amber might look like. A school bag thrown across the floor when your child arrives home. Your child objecting to or criticizing lots of little things over several hours or days. Or weeks or months when everything is a source of tension. Taken a bit further, it's your child actively finding fault with all the little things and looking out for them. Their hoodie hasn't been cleaned, their food or cutlery is 'wrong', they can't find something they really need but haven't *actually* looked for, we are wearing something they consider objectionable, we're walking too close or not close enough to them, they ask for something that they know we will absolutely say no to. Usually, these complaints and criticisms are delivered with some level of venom or contempt, or anger and I term this behaviour *picking a fight*. Our job is to deftly and concertedly *not* pick up the gauntlet. Amber might also look like yelling, swearing, spitting (like the way male footballers do as opposed to spitting at us or someone else), sulking around us, invading our personal space, puffing themselves up, goading us, making fun of us, using terms or language that offend us such as racist or sexist words or phrases. It might involve slamming doors or rough handling of any item, threats, being in the same room as you on a video or loudspeaker call with a friend, talking loudly about something or some drama they know you won't like.

Play and our states

While it's true that our nervous system allows for 'flow' of transition between states, some of us do have less flow than others and a tendency to super-charge into flight, fight or freeze. One reason for that might have a strong link to our opportunity to play as a child. In babies, games like peek-a-boo, round-and-round the garden and crawl-chase (when you get on all fours and 'chase' your baby, in my case while saying something like 'I'm coming!' in a 'Heeeeeere's Johnny!' kind of tone without the definite intent to brutally murder) are developmentally really important. If you have ever played such games with a baby/toddler or watched this happening, you will have quickly noticed the way the baby changes their breathing (faster and more from the chest), giggles nervously in anticipation and squeals with joy at the moment of, 'Boo!', 'Tickly under there!' or 'Gotcha!'

You will also notice how conflicted some of those responses are. There is a mixture of happiness and fun alongside nervousness and jumps of surprise. When children are older, they play sardines, catch/tag and hide-and-seek to name a few. Again, these games have the same conflicting elements. They also have conflicting mobilization states: the still fixation on the parent as they wait for the Boo! and when it comes, jumping in surprise; the ability to stay very quiet and still in their hiding place while holding on to enormous anticipation about being found. What happens through play such as this is that we become good at moving between our states. In all these games, we are in 'safe and social' state but learn to tolerate feelings of danger and the need to run or hide.

Sadly, when we do not experience these intersubjective, relational games, we don't develop the same capacity for deftly navigating between our states and it follows then that holding confusion, misunderstanding, a neutral face, banter, or hearing 'No' in multiple states might be very difficult. When we have not had the chance to exercise 'state-to-state muscles' we're not so great at moving between them in a fluid or nuanced way. So next time you're playing with a baby or watching children play, you can feel safe in the knowledge that those kids are literally gaining regulatory capacity, learning to hold emotional tension and learning to be curious about other people's states and intentions.

TIP
Embrace play no matter their age

How do we increase playful capacity in older children? We need to play to their developmental age and not their chronological one. Regression can be highly therapeutic too, so don't be afraid to get out the play dough, add loads of bubbles to their bath or watch cartoons with your 15-year-old. If you have the space and resources, huge hammocks or swinging chairs in the garden that you can share with your child or push them in are great, too.

When they need to fight

When our child is heading towards fight or teetering around the boundary between 'okay' and 'fighty' we first must be able to identify that this is where they are. We spoke in Chapter 4 about this. That comes with time and remaining curious and observant about your child's behaviours and what these are conveying about their internal state. Sometimes we read this brilliantly, employ one or a number of the approaches below and it still goes tits up and bottomed out. Sometimes, our kids *need* the fight. They want either you or them to explode to somehow exorcise the rage they feel, to purge the pain and puke out the pus of provocation that is organizing them. When it goes like this, often the things we try to avoid the violence isn't enough and we need to be kind to ourselves about that, whether it was us who blew or our child. It's important that we, as adults, aren't the ones to lose it but if we do, we can be kind to ourselves and take the opportunity to reflect and repair with our child: 'I feel that when it went wrong earlier and I yelled, you really needed someone to do the yelling/anger. I'm sorry I let your anger become my anger. I'm working on that.'

When it happens again we can name it: [with matching affect] 'It feels as if you really want me to do your anger for you! That's why you keep asking me stuff you know I can't do/agree to' or, 'I'm not doing your anger for you. You need to talk to me about how you're feeling rather than trying to make me explode.'

The Squirrel

There are a few funny scenes in the animated film, *Up*, where there are dogs who have been fitted with collars that allow their thoughts to be translated into human speech. Several times, mid-dialogue and mid-dastardly plotting, the dogs rapidly turn their heads and say 'Squirrel!' because they are completely unable to resist the distraction of a squirrel. Having recently acquired a rescue dog for my son, I am frequently exposed to the power of the squirrel when I walk the dog. 'The Squirrel' is a distraction technique that sometimes works when children are in the Amber Zone. For my daughter, realizing that there is a football game available to watch on television will bring her swiftly out of any surly mood-hole she may be in. For other children, it might be: 'Shall we walk to the shops and get an ice-cream...it feels like an ice-cream kind of day!' Or, 'Oh, it's Auntie Wendy's birthday soon! Let's go online and choose her a present!' Or, 'Oh no, the dog's almost run out of treats. Let's walk to the pet shop and get some.'

If you can include any form of exercise or getting outside in your Squirrel move, double points for you. Both those things are great for shaking off angst in any form. Now, I want to be clear...distraction is *not* about avoiding feelings. No, no. The very fabric of my job is helping children to stay with difficult feelings without becoming overwhelmed by them. Feelings must be felt and processed forever and always, Amen. Distraction is about avoiding violence. You, as the sentient adult to your child, may choose to return to the reason for the Amber-like behaviours later that evening or the following day – in fact, I would encourage this. You can be curious and warm and empathic about the 'wobble' they had and discuss it when they're in the Green Zone. Does this risk putting them back into Amber? For some kids, yes, but at least you'll be ready for it so can time this well and deliver your curiosity in a helpful place like in a car or on a walk (see Chapter 7 on how to deliver a 'No' – same principles apply).

TIP

Write a list of pre-prepared distractions.

Drag them into consciousness

When I am in a session with a child and their parents/carers, an important aspect of my work is to create a sense of safety for everyone in the room. When talking about something difficult, a child will, of course, become defensive. They may shift states or start heading to the edges of their capacity. The less capacity they have, the less conscious they become. That might sound dramatic, but the truth is that in the face of stress, exposure, life threat or danger, our brains prioritize survival over 'thrival' (a word that Sally and I would like to see added to the dictionary) and in that state, consciousness becomes superfluous to requirements. Part of my approach with families is to keep consciousness online. An important way that we do this is to say or do something unexpected or surprising. Neuroscientist and author, David Eagleman[3] talks about how, when we see something unexpected like a person dressed as a massive bee walking down the high street, our brains are forced to examine what is happening with our conscious brain. For our children, that might mean us being really nice when they're being pretty vile or giving them truckloads of empathy about a situation or being angry (in a controlled way) about something they are angry about. It can literally slow their ramping-up brains down.

Tone is everything

We've all heard that the spoken word is only a small amount of all our communication (about 7%) and the rest is non-verbal. But of the remaining 93%, about 38% is vocal, which includes inflection and tone of voice. The tone of our voice can be used in so many ways and is crucial in the application of PACE (playfulness, acceptance, curiosity, empathy), one aspect of the dyadic developmental psychotherapy approach I practise. When we as humans are experiencing stress or danger/life threat, our brains do an incredible thing. Rather than make its usual pathway from aural stimulus to a response, it actually takes a longer detour to an area of the brain responsible for language and tonal recognition (Broca's Wernicke's, for anatomy fans). There, it turns *down* the language processing and, you guessed it, turns *up* the tone processing. All humans, but particularly traumatized ones, are predisposed to interpret lower vocal tones as threatening. It follows that when we are engaging with children in the Amber Zone, it helps to try to keep our tone of voice in the mid and upper ranges. It also helps to keep our faces fairly positive-looking too. Just like our voices, our faces will be scanned by our children and much of the time, neutral faces will be interpreted as negative. In nervous state terms, when we are in safety, we engage in eye contact, we smile, our eyes smile too with their shape and the way the skin crinkles around them and the position of our eyebrows.

TIP

Practise talking to your child when they aren't around. Notice the tone of your voice, especially when you are riled or addled. You could even look in the mirror and practise maintaining a positive face. You'll be surprised at how easily we convey negativity even when we don't mean to.

When our child is in Amber, we are trying to convey safe tones with a face that matches. Think Drag Queen or Pantomime Dame. High eyebrows, keen interest in your child conveyed in your eyes, a slight smile where appropriate. It's very difficult to 'write' the kinds of tones I mean. But I'll try. When your child is on the up, you could try these:

The hold your horses
'Wow, you are *aaaa*ngry! What's up, I want to know?!'

'Whoa whoa whoa, talk to me, talk to me!'

The firm but fair

'I can see you're *really* wound up and I want to talk but I'm *not* for swearing at.'

'Stop hitting. I'm right here. You are *safe*.'

'I will discuss this but *not now*. We're both wound up; let's get some air.'

The playful

'I can't hear you when you're shouting!'

'Wow, I must have made your sandwiches *really* badly for you to be this angry with me!'

The nonchalant (but not sarcastic)

(Usually in response to something you really *do* care about like your child telling you they're going to dye their hair a hideous colour or they're going to call Childline or you look shit in that brand-new dress you just bought.)

'Okay, love. If you want to talk about it, that's fine.'

'Aww, do you reckon? That's entirely up to you. Thanks for giving me your opinion.'

The sliding scale

(Here you start by matching their emotional tone and then kind of reducing the volume and intensity to something more pianissimo or affective (feeling-y).)

'Oh my gosh, that sounds like it's made you *soooo angry*! That is *sooo rubbish* that the teacher made you feel that way! I bet you wanted to just *get up and walk out*. Phew, you did *so* well not to. You know what...(short pause)...you did *really* well not to walk out. That's *such* good self-control so maybe now you just needed to let a bit of steam off. I get it. You really did your best today. How about a hot chocolate and a hug?'

The genuine empathy

(Must be conveyed with absolute feeling for your child and the experience they're having.)

'Oh, lovey, that must have been so hard for you/that sounds so difficult. Is that right, does it feel hard? You just wanted Lily to be your friend and she wouldn't let you play in her group. You must have felt so small and sad when she said no. Maybe how it's been since you got home is because you've been holding in those big feelings all day...'

Say less

Having said all of that, we also have found that there are times when our children are in Amber and keeping schtum is the most helpful course of action, especially when we can feel our child picking a fight or goading us. Remaining tight-lipped here isn't about us being submissive, it's about us maintaining the control when we are being invited to fight or sabotage what was quite a nice day until that point. Saying less is also connected to the importance of reading where your child is at to help manage how we parent them. It's strongly advised that if our children are in the Amber Zone we take care not to make any demands when they are teetering on fight, such as, 'Put your shoes away', 'Hang your coat up'. This often can turn into 'walking on eggshells' but if the child can harness some of our own confidence and physical mobilization then we can avoid this. Plenty of doing rather than saying can demonstrate safe proximity – hanging their coat up, making them a sandwich, doing them some toast. These acts are doubly helpful because they enable mobilized listening as well, which is safer for us. As parents, many of us have natural, connecting curiosity about how our child's day in school has been. How was your test? Who did you play with? Was Mr Gerrish at gardening club? Did you feel safe? Often this is *the last thing* our kids want to talk about when they get home from school. We might need to get better at picking our curious moments and reading our children's non-verbals.

A reminder about precious things

As per Chapter 3, when things are Amber, consider if there is anything that needs hiding or protecting in case Amber turns to raging Red. Hopefully it won't, but let's play safe and if we *do* feel that moving certain items is a good idea, try to do this in a stealthy manner as your child seeing you take such precautions could escalate them further. I hope

I didn't just sound too much like Boris Johnson mid-Covid advice and guidance...

Flight safety

Now, let's think back again to our states and remind ourselves crucially that when it comes to our nervous systems, we go through flight *before* fight. It therefore follows that if we can promote flight, we stand a better chance of avoiding fight. I therefore recommend the following strategies.

Modelling flight safety

'I'm getting cross; I'm going to step outside for a minute to get some air/I need to walk around the block because I don't want to start shouting. I will be back.'

Creating flight safety

Is there somewhere or someone whom your child perceives as safe and they can run to when things get heated? This will have been discussed with your child (and, where applicable, the adult they can run to) while in the Green Zone.

Follow-me flight safety

Many children who are aggressive/violent under distress cannot bear distance from us in Amber or Red Zones even though everything about them appears to want this. Otherwise, why would they be attacking us? But the ambivalent push-you-pull-you or the 'I hate you, don't leave me' dynamic of anger tells us that some level of distance is helpful without making it absolute. That might be, 'I'm going for a walk around the block, and you can follow me round' or, 'I'm going for a walk around the block so we can walk and talk'.

Here-not-here flight safety

This is very similar to the 'Follow-me' method above but still inside the home. Your child needs space but needs to know you are still there. This involves you saying, 'I'm stepping outside this room, but I'll be just outside' or, 'I'm going to give you some space but I'm not going anywhere' as you back away from them but to a nearby distance.

Food

This works a bit like 'The Squirrel' but also has a sensory dimension to it. Food is *very* important to most children who have a history of trauma but given how vital it is for our survival, it usually carries an emotional element for most of us. Sensory experts tell us that when we are anxious, we should eat something crunchy and when we are angry, we should eat something chewy. When our children come in from school in an agitated state, frankly I'm not sure the texture is as important as getting something into them. Often I have found that only something the child views as a 'treat' will stand a chance of getting them closer to the Green Zone.

TIP

Always leave the house with 'emergency foods' stashed in a pocket or bag.

Sometimes the Amber Zone can last a long time, over many days and it's as much as we can do to get through each day until our child is asleep. Some parents talk about their child waking up in the Amber Zone. Some have followed advice about giving their child a square of dark chocolate as soon as they wake up as it can have a mood-stabilizing effect on the hippocampus (see Appendix A), but I don't know anyone who has continued long term with this practice so I'm not sure about its efficacy. There is every possibility that waking up in the Amber Zone is more about dreading the day that's coming, or even anger that their sleep, which has been a welcome reprieve from themselves and their life, is over. I don't believe our children want to wake up angry and rarely do they want to be angry at all. And yet it takes so much of themselves and so much of us to signpost, drag, pave the way, invite them in, bribe, bundle and claw their way back towards the Green Zone. That is surely a testament to the powerful protective nature of our nervous systems.

CHAPTER 6

Becoming a Stress Detective

—— Sally ——

W hen lives are dominated by violent waves, how is it possible to regain a footing and prevent family lives from being washed away? It may feel like a most unappealing prospect, but one of the answers is to turn detective and carry out some problem-solving.

Problem-solving is a gold-standard parenting skill and as such we get it wrong as much as we get it right. And sometimes there just isn't a neat answer, or at least if there is we can't see it. But we may just make some sense of the chaos. We can then begin to unpick the root causes, put in some preventative measures and give ourselves and our families some breathing space. With breathing space comes the energy to tackle the more difficult challenges (education, getting help) and to invest in our own lives and happiness. Making sense reaps other rewards too – it leads us in the direction of empathy (my child and I are not to blame) and agency (I can do something about this).

To begin to make sense of a violent incident, we want to pose some questions:

- What led up to the incident?

- Was there an identifiable, defined event?

- Was there a more general build-up of stress?

- Is it more complicated than that?

These are questions that we will have to sit with and not rush at and which will need to hang in the air for a while.

> **TIP**
> **If the last thing you feel like doing is problem-solving your life...**
>
> If you are in a place of anger, bitterness, vengefulness, hopelessness and exhaustion, you may see my footprints in the earth beneath you, because I've been to that place many times.
>
> This is what I have learned.
>
> Wallow in whatever you need to wallow in – blame, self-pity, whatever. Self-medicate on junk food and junk TV, vent, swear, cry and wail.
>
> Close this book.
>
> Stop listening to the well-meaning advice.
>
> Leave the hard work for another day.
>
> Your future self is up to the job.
>
> Your current self needs a break.

Problem-solving is a cognitive process and our cognitive skills are impaired when we are scared, angry, frustrated or otherwise stressed. I have had to put time aside for this kind of problem-solving, in an intentional way, as in, 'I can't think about this now, but I've got a one-hour window later this afternoon.'

Problem-solving time can involve some kind of activity like walking or sweeping the floor, that doesn't take too much concentration and allows the mind to roam. It may be that staring at the walls does the job just as well. Sometimes I've reached for a pen and allowed the frustrations, fears and angers to flood out in a completely unstructured way. Dumping everything on paper can make sense of the tangled mess. It's also cathartic.

Physical distance from the house and from the violence can be helpful but isn't always possible. For some, letting go of anger is almost impossible when 'at the scene of the crime'. And it may be necessary to shake off the untruths one has told oneself – that a loved one is entirely to blame and could decide to stop the behaviour if they chose to and that the adults in the room were entirely faultless. The penny may drop when minds are freed up, calmed and allowed to wander.

When minds have been in a state of overwhelm over a long period of time, figuring out triggers and strategies is better done as a team. You should have a therapist who absolutely gets violent behaviour and therapeutic parenting approaches, who will have these explorative conversations with you and help you put in place strategies that don't involve naughty steps, excluding or taking away nice things. They will also help you to think through your own responses and gently work through some alternatives, without making you feel like a hopeless failure. If you don't have such a therapist, it helps to have someone who 'gets it' – a partner, friend or peer support buddy. Without such a 'critical friend', who is able to challenge you without making you feel like a failure, or sending you to a defensive position, there is a risk of getting locked into anger and a gnawing sense of unfairness.

Our children are likely to find it difficult to identify what it was that sparked a violent incident or run of incidents. They will be contending with mammoth amounts of shame and most likely fractured and dislocated memories of an explosive event. We have to do the cognitive work for them, like their second brain. What could the trigger or triggers have been? What strategies, workarounds and solutions might alleviate the trigger in the future? As our children grow older and become more accomplished at reading and sharing their own inner worlds, this is work we can do together – exploring triggers, without shame, and developing coping strategies that eventually our children or young adults can use for themselves. We may start these tentative steps, when all is calm, with: 'Help me understand'. When we can explore and problem-solve together, we're well on our way to making some big improvements. This takes years of careful work and courage.

Understanding triggers not only paves the way to greater understanding, empathy and improvements – it helps us realize that violence usually has a rational cause or set of causes or reasons and doesn't take place because we are uniquely terrible people. Whatever triggers you uncover, you are likely to have to adjust your thinking, approaches and behaviour to reduce their potency or to try and avoid them. You may find yourself thinking back over situations and feel intense, burning shame at how you dealt with them at the time. That is not the same as being a failure as a parent. This is learning from experience. It's what all of us do, whether we are parenting children who are fostered, adopted, bereaved, scared, grieving or living through a hundred other experiences. In this game called Life, we've drawn the card that says, 'You Must Go the Extra Mile'. Whether we chose that card or not, there will always be times of denial, frustration and 'why me?' It's worth remembering that our children won't have chosen the cards that they are holding.

I've listed a few ways of approaching stress detection and problem-solving. It's worth bearing in mind that what we usually know is the headline and what we need to delve into is the detail. It can take a lot of thought to really grasp the root causes.

Right here, right now

Sometimes it's obvious what has sparked an incident. Event A happened and it led to Event B. The treasured mobile phone got broken and then a door was pulled off its hinges. An ice-cream was dropped on the ground and you got thumped in the back. But how come some children can drop an ice-cream and laugh it off while others punch their loved one in the back? It's because we're talking about distressed children who don't yet have a cushion between an accident and feelings of intense pain and shame.

- I dropped my ice cream because I am a hopeless failure.

- I always mess things up.

- I won't get another ice cream.

- Everyone saw me drop my ice cream.

- I was a bit over-excited and dysregulated, and the shock tipped me over.

Our and our child's capacity to cope with these unexpected disappointments isn't static. Some days, when life is cool, our children may surprise us with how well they surf disappointment. Other days, it won't take much to unleash the hounds. It's a bit like how we come to think about biological versus developmental maturity – it's something of a moving feast.

There are some strategies you can try.

Emotional weather forecasting

Sharing our emotional weather with our child and modelling and encouraging good, healthy conversations about how we're feeling can build emotional literacy. 'I'm stressed today and that's why I shouted when I dropped the bottle of cooking oil on the kitchen floor. Another day I would have dealt with that better.' That kind of thing. 'I'm stressed today and might not cope well if anything goes wrong, but I'll try and keep myself to myself until I've shaken this feeling off,' is what we're aiming for. If you're thinking, 'My child would take that as a weakness and exploit it' then perhaps don't go there for now, or use a proxy, such as a character in a film or story as the basis to talk about emotions.

Preparation and empathy

Being prepared for these sorts of sudden disappointments and having a response at your fingertips such as, 'It's okay, I'll buy you another ice-cream,' followed up with, 'You're stressed about a load of stuff and I think that's why the ice-cream tipped you over', can help to demonstrate love and acceptance. Part of the power of therapeutic parenting power is surprising our loved ones in these sorts of positive ways.

Triggers, or if it's hysterical, it's historical

Getting to grips with what triggers an incident is easier if you know some of the neuroscience around threat perception and models of the world. We have set this out in Chapter 4.

If you're dealing with baffling and shocking 'out-of-the-blue' situations, those 'where did *that* come from?' moments, then think *survival* and *triggers*. Crudely speaking, if we once got badly bitten by a white dog, we may tense up, panic, scream, throw our ice-cream or suchlike whenever we see a white dog. If something that appears minor to you results in your child flaring up, it's fair to assume that their threat system did not consider the event to be minor. There is no choice in the matter – that's what bodies do to stay alive. What we are focusing on here is the fight response but you might see other responses such as flight (running), freeze, hiding, dissociation and flopping at other times. All are clues to the Stress Detective.

Our body's threat detection and survival systems aren't only interested in the events we can remember (they are more sophisticated than that) and they are a stickler for detail. They have everything on file, right the way back to our very earliest experiences. That's something I didn't appreciate well enough when my children were small. I wish I had. At that time, there was a queue of people desperate to tell me, 'They're too young to remember!' which roughly translates as, 'They should be all right by now', and by logical extension, 'It must be your parenting that's to blame'. What I didn't know was that our bodies remember it all – whether that's being left alone and in pain with hunger, being screamed at and shamed, being unsafe with adults who smell of alcohol, having a sibling who is unwell and dying, a parent disappearing out of their lives or being bitten by a white dog. The brain flags up any signs that these events or situations are going to take place again, so that this time, the body is primed and ready to keep itself safe. Its job is not to reason with itself. That's why there's no point someone telling a child there's really nothing to shout about. You can take on the body's survival system, but you won't win. Logic is no match for survival. In my experience, survival trumps everything.

Some events might not seem to us like a threat to survival. Take the dropped ice-cream on the sandy pavement example. What if the child has experienced hunger, or learned that attracting attention leads to abuse? Or if the situation mainlines straight to feelings of overwhelming shame, or fear that an adult will walk away? Instead of arguing with the body's survival systems, we are aiming to calm our child and help them feel safe and ultimately to help them make sense of what's going on.

Here are some strategies to try.

Joint problem-solving

Narrating what has happened and thinking out loud can help adults and children to come up with solutions together. These can work far better than an idea that's got ADULT stamped all over it, especially for children who need some control. 'I might be wrong but I think I've noticed that your behaviour wobbles when I've drunk some alcohol', can be a way of approaching these sorts of conversations. Or, 'I think I've spotted a pattern. Sunday evenings are difficult. What's that about?'

Joining the dots

We can help our children to make sense of their inner world and reduce feelings of shame with conversation starters like: 'You really panicked when you dropped the ice-cream. I wonder if you thought you were in trouble?' and 'You looked so worried when I was late to pick you up from school. Perhaps deep inside you didn't trust I would come at all?'

Sensory triggers

Our experiences are powerfully tied in to our sensory world. Threatening situations don't play out in sterile, blank spaces, but in environments rich in smells, tastes, sounds, sensations and visual images. The senses are our navigational tools and send us messages from the past. The smells of a hospital ward or school dinners are like sensory time machines. If these time machines transport us back to a time when we were unsafe, our flight, fight and freeze response may be primed for action.

This kind of response used to be referred to as something that took place in the 'base', 'primitive' or 'reptilian' brain, as opposed to the 'mammalian' or 'higher' brain, which was concerned with clever stuff like algebra. There seems to be a move away from such hierarchical reptile versus mammal brain talk, towards something more integrated and, let's face it, a little more respectful of the wonders of the human body. Using terms like 'primitive' risks seeing children who act out of survival as rather unevolved. There has also been some suggestion that one can switch between one's 'primitive' and 'thinking' brains, with a bit of grit and effort. I'd say this is a dubious assertion.

Let's think about some of the sensory triggers that might be buried in your family life, waiting to fire off like land mines. It's impossible to capture this vast subject here, so these are a starter for ten.

Smells

A particular soap, washing powder or perfume all have the power to comfort or alarm. That distinctive hospital smell, the whiff of dirty laundry, of faeces, alcohol, tobacco may all have a mess of memories woven into them. Children with experience of not feeling safe in their early lives seem to have an enhanced sense of smell. They can literally smell out danger and comfort and can even tell you whose school jumper belongs to whom, by smell alone.

Sounds

Raised voices, loud music, sirens, a dog barking may all be sensory alarm signals. Children may detect danger in the faintest faraway noise, like an exhaust backfiring. When the body has learned that the world is not safe, it tunes itself incredibly finely. 'Don't shout at me!' your child may yell, when you've asked them to put a plate in the dishwasher. They are more likely to detect threat in what is a non-threatening situation, than someone who has learned that the world is generally a safe place to be.

Sensations

Being wet, cold, overheated, hungry or in pain are powerful sensations that may transport a child back in time. You may not notice they are uncomfortable or in pain and they may not know they are either. When children have experienced overwhelming pain, discomfort and fear, the body has a way of severing the consciousness from the physical body. The proper name for this is dissociation. If you have a child who disso-ciates, you may have to work extra hard to figure out what their sensory triggers are and to help them to build body awareness.

Sights

An angry, disgusted or irritated facial expression, a face reminiscent of another time, an arm suddenly raised, a syringe, medicines, alcohol, blood, a paint colour, a lampshade can all signal extreme danger. Objects that to most adults might appear quite neutral and 'other' may be drip-ping with personal trauma triggers to children with a history of trauma.

Tastes

The taste of blood is one of the most powerful sensory triggers I've witnessed. Mouldy food, vomit and medicines can also signal a lack of safety.

Starting to think about and identify sensory triggers allows us to wonder, to ourselves and when the time is right, out loud with our child. We may then have to build things into our day to avoid these sensory triggers, if we can, for instance by having plentiful food available at hungry times of the day, such as the return home from school, and by experimenting with washing powders and soaps.

Seasonal triggers

The seasons can play a particularly potent role in our children's inner lives and are of course sensory triggers. Many parents and carers will be familiar with repeating patterns of rising tension and increased stress over time. It seems that the timing of a stressful event, or set of events, is an important part of the record that our bodies keep. The smells, temperature and general feel of a season can take children back to a time when life was tough and dangerous. You may notice them becoming more volatile just as spring starts and green smells emerge, or when the sun is high in the sky and the air is dusty, or with the spicy, boozy smells and music of Christmas. When our children are old enough to understand, we may begin to make sense of this for and with them: 'I've noticed that April is always a difficult month. Maybe the smells and sounds of April take you back to that time. What can we do to make April a little easier?' These are among the most powerful conversations we can have. Until we can have them, we may have to predict difficult times ahead and ease back on commitments where we can.

Pressure building up like a volcano

While some incidents have a clear(ish), clean(ish) cause and effect and are over and done with fairly swiftly, there may be situations that build and boil over time. You spot dark clouds gathering way off on the horizon. The light changes. The birds tweet anxiously and take to the trees. A wind kicks up. The sky grows darker. You know for sure there is going to be a heck of a storm, you just don't know when it will hit. You start to think it'll be a relief when it does, just so it can be over with.

While detecting the warning signs isn't pleasant, if we can recognize them, we at least have some opportunity to try and work out what is going on. You may notice some of the following: exchanges become snappy and fractious, arguments take place over tiny things, body language changes, there are problems at school, self-care slips, sleep becomes disturbed, your child is more sensitive and easily wounded than usual, they are generally dysregulated, have a reduced capacity to cope with disappointment or failure, they skulk or creep around the home. You will get a growing sense of dread and doom that violence is about to break out in your home.

If you are completely baffled by the cause of the stress, I would first ask this – does the cause lie at home, or is it being imported from elsewhere? Children can hold in stress for long periods of time, especially when they don't feel safe enough to expose their distress. They clamp it down until they are in a safe place, with adults who they know aren't going to reject them. When it's impossible for them to hold it in any longer, it spills out. School stress is the classic of this genre.

Here are some examples of situations that may lead to a long, drawn-out and dreaded build-up of stress:

- A significant transition.

- Friendship problems.

- Fear of a lie or misdemeanour being uncovered.

- Bullying.

- Getting into trouble on social media.

- End of school term exhaustion.

- Dreading something.

Strategies to try:

- Wonder out loud: 'I think I might have worked something out. Could the stress be about falling out with your friend?'

- Permission for self-care: 'You look so tired. We're going to take a day off school and spend some quiet time together.'

- Permission for difficult feelings: 'It's so hard when we dread something. I'd be a bit scared about that too.' Pause. 'And it's still not okay to hurt me.'

Releasing stress in a safe place

Most of us show ourselves in all our complicated, messy, imperfect glory to our loved ones, in our places of safety. Sometimes children show anger and violence at home, because that's where they feel safe to do so. What they often can't do is tell the adults around them the reasons why. The shame associated with an incident might be too massive and overwhelming to share. There may even be an underlying fear that if they share a deeply shameful experience, we might reject them as well. Many of our children are operating on flimsier foundations. Their 'go to' might be, 'I am that pathetic and useless person. It is my fault. Everyone can see my failings. I will be rejected'. This is why efforts to get inside their world and empathize with their feelings are so key to tackling violent and aggressive behaviour. It is also why acting contrary to the way they expect us to, is one of the best tools at our disposal.

'What a massive jerk that person was to you.'

'That would have upset me too.'

'That must have felt awful.'

When we can identify some of the triggers, or combinations or layers of triggers, we can begin the important task of working out what to do with that information. The clues will be there somewhere, and if they aren't, we may have to take a punt. Sometimes stress detective work involves taking small risks but it gets easier with experience, for us and for our child.

One of the most significant and powerful triggers I have witnessed is a single word. The mayhem that this word can unleash is incredible. If your stress detectoring has identified the same trigger in your home, then head for Chapter 7, which is devoted entirely to the word 'no'.

CHAPTER 7

The Art of Saying 'No'

—— Sally ——

In tinder-dry home environments, a tiny spark can result in a raging forest fire. The language chosen, or sometimes not chosen (when it comes tumbling out of our mouths) can create those tiny sparks. One of the most incendiary of all the sparks is a tiny and yet powerful two-lettered word – 'no'.

Being told that 'no', they can't do whatever it is they have locked their sights on to, can be one of the biggest triggers we can stumble on, sending our children straight into a flight or fight situation. One sign that 'no' is too hot to handle in our homes is when we find ourselves avoiding it – saying 'yes' when we mean 'no', or not saying anything at all and hoping that somehow everything will work out. As saying 'yes' to every question and demand isn't practical or safe, and doesn't always work out that well either, the stinging nettle of 'no' has got to be grasped.

Ultimately, as parents and carers we are equipping our children to function in the big wide world and that big wide world delivers a fair few 'nos'. Learning to hear 'no' and process let down and disappointment is a life skill.

When we share our lives with a child who can be violent, there is a subtle and sometimes not so subtle shift in the power balance. We're never going to be able to parent by force and control (can you even imagine how that would turn out?) but there are nevertheless situations when adults have to take charge and do what's in the best interests of children. I know, right! Whatever next?

Trying to exercise assertiveness is no easy feat when living in a state of fear. It can lead to a lot of second guessing, over-thinking and a lack of practice. The underlying fear may leak out through attempts at assertiveness, making it seem not quite believable and this can further dysregulate an already dysregulated child. Traumatized children simultaneously need adults to be both weak and dominated by their immediate needs, and strong. They become dysregulated by seeing their parents and carers weakened and therefore unlikely to be strong enough to keep them safe, and by them demonstrating their strength and protectiveness. They need them to say 'no' and yet hate them for saying it. It's what's known as a 'no-win situation'. In this line of parenting, there are a lot of those. What one can become proficient in is seeking out the least shit option. The Least Shit Option could be the subtitle of this chapter.

I'm going to share with you a number of ways I found of saying 'no' without the roof falling in. It might be more accurate to say 'without the roof falling in some of the time'.

How not to say 'no'

Starting with a negative is not ideal, but let's get this out of the way. The negative 'no' is a direct route to shame, and shame as we know is a direct route to the threat detection system and its 'fightiness'. The shameful 'no' goes something like this:

- 'No, because you are too young to do that.'

- 'No, because you will break it.'

- 'No, because can you remember the disaster last time you went there?'

All of these 'no, because' phrases are laced with shame – you are a bad child, who fails at everything. This is not what we are aiming for. This kind of no is a great big trigger.

We've all blurted out a negative 'no' at some time or another. On the page, they look pretty awful but when we employ them there may well have been a context. The context may be anything from your own parents, carers or teachers speaking to you like this when you were young, to this being question number 150 of the day and it's only 7.30 in the morning.

What follows is a selection of ways of approaching 'no' in a kind and assertive manner. It looks easy. It isn't. Strategies must be chosen while we are possibly being bombarded with reasons why the only option we have is to say 'yes' and that 'no' is going to ruin everything. For that reason, I recommend having a few strategies practised in your imaginary parenting world and ready for when you need them.

> ## TIP
> ## The Mental Practice Court of Parenting
>
> When we live in fast-moving, fractious and heated homes, it is important to set aside time for mental preparation. Allowing the mind to wander around, think through possible scenarios and try out different responses and strategies can get us ready and fit for future conflict.
>
> If this happened, what would I do?
>
> If they responded this way, what would be my reply?
>
> Play out situations in your mind and you'll be able to reach for them when and if they take place in real life. It's a bit like developing mental muscle memory.

The buy-yourself-time no

This is perhaps the most useful of all the no strategies and it goes like this:

> 'I wasn't expecting that question. I'm going to take some time to think about it.'
>
> 'Thanks for asking. I'll get back to you on that.'
>
> 'Good question. Not sure right now.'

You know the kinds of phrases that work best in your home, but you get the idea. If some of the more 'therapy-friendly' phrasing irritates the situation, you may have to be more direct and choose language which is yours and not someone else's. Something like, 'I'm so impressed you've asked me. Thank you. I'm going to think really hard about how to answer you because you deserve it' certainly has its merits, but many of us are way too far gone to manage it with any authenticity. Forcing something faux-therapeutic out of our mouths can enrage us as well as our already enraged child.

The buy-yourself-time no slows down an exchange and reduces the likelihood that we are bounced into a decision we may later regret.

A simple question such as: 'Can I stay at Lucy's tonight?' may be way more complicated to answer in our homes than in others. There are going to be many factors to consider. Will Lucy's parents be at home? Will Lucy's much older brother be there? Who even is Lucy? We need our cognitive faculties to work on this, and not our fighty, panicky, inflexible ones.

The buy-yourself-time no may need reinforcing, especially if your child usually benefits from keeping the tempo high and rushing you into panicked decisions. You are gently taking back some control and they may not respond well. The power balance may mean that you have had little control of late and it may freak everyone out, including you.

'Woah. I'm just taking a breath here.'

'My brain needs time.'

You may need to remove yourself to avoid being trampled by the hooves of urgency. You may find some essential laundry that needs folding, remember the bins need bringing in, or you may think you heard a knock at the door that needs investigating. Keeping active and mobile in such situations can keep our stress levels under control and ease our thinking.

The ante may get upped in ways such as, 'You told me I could, don't you remember?' or, 'You've met Lucy and you liked her'. Very clever? But did you really? In my world, possibly not. I'm the kind of person that likes to say a big fat 'YES' to social things so I guess this was always going to be my weakness. My keenness probably gave me away from time to time. It's not great to point this out, but a dysregulated child, desperate to have a particular need met, right *now* is adept at reading us. They see the indecision in our eyes and hear the floundering in our voices. The only way I know of fortifying ourselves is to be aware of our own weak points. Who exactly do I want this for? Is this my stuff or theirs? The buy-yourself-time no is a way of re-centring and inviting our rational selves back into the room.

Did I meet Lucy? No, I didn't. Do I know where she lives? Again, no. Would I like my child to have a lovely friend who they can have drama-free sleepovers with? Of course, I would. But that's not where we are right now. Let's take this more slowly.

A quick note about The Galloping Hooves of Urgency
In our families, we develop ways of describing things that 'normal' families don't generally experience and therefore don't need to describe. Railroading is a good term, if your loved one understands what that is. You may have to come up with something that they 'get' and which can become part of your family lexicon.

'I see what's going on, you're trying to railroad me.'

'Is that the Galloping Hooves of Urgency I hear?'

'This conversation is moving quickly!'

This naming of terms and exploring what they mean is carried out when everyone is regulated and it's done with curiosity. 'I've noticed that when you want something badly, you speak really quickly and give me lots of information.' You may want to act this out to add extra colour.

Is it really a no?
Living with extreme stress and high risk can cause us to become inflexible and negative. This is not because we are awful, inflexible and negative people by nature, it is because this is what happens to humans living under these conditions. It is our biology. 'No' is part of the quick-fire, trigger-happy *fight* armoury. It comes out of our mouths before we've even had time to consider. And we may have got used to saying 'no' to a stream of unmeetable demands. It becomes a habit. If it's any consolation, it's the same for our children. Will they please put their shoes on? Will they take a shower? Will they clear up the kitchen? Absolutely flippin' not. NO!

Again, in order to think about whether a 'no' is really a 'yes' we need time and a breather. We need to regulate ourselves, before we reason with ourselves. Deploy the buy-yourself-time no and ask yourself, can I say 'yes' to this request? Is it that outlandish? What's the worst that can possibly happen here?

You may be able to scratch around for a partial 'yes'. A partial 'yes' might sound like, 'You can go for the evening and I'll pick you up before bedtime'. If the partial 'yes' releases the hounds of wrath, then you may need to be ready with a, 'I know you want to stay over but that's my best offer'.

A place where 'no' can get to be a very worn-out word is the super-market. 'Can I have this?' All children do it, of course, particularly toddlers. The supermarket toddler meltdown is a classic of the genre; the adolescent supermarket meltdown less so. If you absolutely have to go to the supermarket with your angry adolescent, then this pre-shop briefing may help.

> 'You're going to want to ask me for loads of things, and I get that and it's fine. Because I can't say "yes" to everything, you can choose one thing from the sweet aisle.'

We're not meant to bribe our children to behave, are we? All I'll say is we are way off normal parenting here. What we're doing is getting the 'yes' in ahead of time. We are giving our child some control. It means we are setting the tone and taking charge. It's also a way of demonstrating that we know our child well and can see into their world, and that's a very powerful thing. If on the other hand, nothing makes going to the supermarket anything other than a hellish experience, don't go with them. End of.

The thinking-out-loud no

You will have practised your thinking-out-loud no on your mental prac-tice court of parenting (see previous tip). This is rather a performance, but avoids a straight-up 'no' and seeks to lay the path for a resolution. You can be playful with this and 'in it together' even though for you it may be an absolute 'no way, ever'. It's about voicing our thought process, or rather a more organized version of it. It shows we are considering all sides and options and it models good problem-solving skills.

> 'What happened last time? I can't quite remember. Ah yes. I'm not sure that's the right thing to do.'

> 'We could open the box of cakes now and eat them all, just you and me. I'd enjoy doing that with you. I'm just thinking about the party later. It wouldn't be great, a party with no cake.'

A quick note about the cake scenario. You'll know whether there is a compromise to be reached with the cakes. Some of our children may be delighted and satisfied to be able to eat one of the cakes ahead of time.

It may be that once the seal on the cake box has been broken, it's open season. You'd better lock those babies somewhere extremely secure, or buy some more. The reason we may have to be more inflexible than our parenting friends is because flexibility can let in dysregulation and that causes conflict.

> 'We're going to save the cakes for later. Yes, I'll make sure you get your fair share.'

Notice there another canny language trick – expressing what is actually a negative, as a positive. It's not 'no you can't have a cake now', but rather 'we're going to save them for later'. When we get good at this, almost every negative can be phrased positively. Clearly, we need to be on top of our game to achieve this kind of parenting wizardry.

TIP
Be flexible on your terms

To keep things on track in our homes we may have to parent in a more predictable and structured way than our friends. To outside eyes, this can appear inflexible and mean.

'Go on, let her have another packet of crisps.'

'Why can't he stay up for another half an hour?'

'The fair is perfectly safe; why don't you trust him to go with his friends?'

If flexibility risks creating dysregulation in your home, be clear and stick to your guns. Experiment with greater flexibility on your terms, in a planned manner, when you have the headspace to prepare your child and the energy to mopup the possible fallout.

The joint-problem-solving no
This is a technique that may ease a deadlock with older children. Again, it's something we will be regulated and prepared for. It may not always work and may fail more often than not. Occasionally, it avoids a full-on confrontation.

The joint-problem-solving no says we're in this together and I'm going to try my best to find a resolution that a) allows you to do whatever it is you want to do; b) keeps you safe; c) depending on the situation, doesn't bankrupt me; d) keeps others safe; e) prevents me from losing my marbles with worry.

Here we go:

'We need to work out a way you can do that successfully.'

'Does it have to be at that time?'

'Let's think about whether there's another way that could work?'

If the child goes into rigid mode, you may need to step away and offer to return to the conversation later. It's a sign of developing maturity if they can quietly seethe and gather themselves together sufficiently enough to try again. They are learning that getting their needs met might involve a bit of discussion and patience, rather than aggression. It will take them time to learn this and it can be a painful and frustrating process for them and for you. Again, we are teaching them skills for the future.

A note about rage (ours)

From time to time it can feel infuriating that we have to go through this kind of head-scrambling rigmarole to teach our child what seem like basic skills of give-and-take and courtesy. Logically, we know that for whatever reason, our child doesn't yet have the skills and so it's up to us to teach them and yet it's really difficult. In fact, it can feel like a total arse-ache. It's perfectly reasonable, and I think necessary, to acknowledge the difficulty and the rage, off-camera and away from our loved ones. 'Why is everything *so* difficult?' will be engraved on my tombstone.

The diverting no

This can be employed to head off the disastrous playdate, party, youth club outing or, 'in extremis', a gathering organized by local drug dealers in a muddy field somewhere no one is entirely sure of. It is a devious kind of 'no', but because it is all about avoiding a complete shitshow, it is for the greater good. It goes like this:

'We've already got something arranged for that day.'

You must then hurriedly think of something, or ideally have something to hand for these types of situations. The something arranged will be an outing that your child will *love* and *not want to miss*. It will have been arranged as a special surprise that you were planning to tell them about this very evening.

'We've got tickets for [film, show or attraction].'

'We're going to [favourite destination].'

'We're having a meal at [favourite place].'

As your incredible surprise is being celebrated, you must then sneak away and arrange it.

When times are becoming really quite risky for your older child, when their spare time is being filled with risk, you may be able to book just a few cheap weekends away to give them temporary respite and to remind them that you are present in their lives, enjoyable to be around and care about them. It's difficult to gather the will to carry this out when you live in a war zone, but in my experience, that's precisely when we should consider deploying nice and unconditional surprises.

The no that sounds like a yes

The no that sounds like a yes is partly a language device and essentially a way of thinking.

'It may be possible on a different day.'

'I could stretch to a reconditioned one.'

'I know how important it is to you. Let's see if we can find a way.'

We are as usual balancing our child's desire with their safety and of course the needs of everyone else in the household, including us. It can be used to engage in a bit of bargaining.

'I'm tired so I can't safely pick you up that late. I'm prepared to come earlier.'

You may be tired because your child stays up late, talks loudly on their device, leaves the lights on, cooks up a meal that you then clear up.

'If you keep the noise down tonight, I'll think about whether it's a "yes".'

It can be tricky making something conditional and we are often advised not to do this. In my world, if you're capable of heading off to someone's house with your hair done and your best outfit on and you can be lovely to their parents, you can jolly well not keep me awake until the early hours of the morning. It comes down to that power balance again. We must not feel compelled to agree to everything just to keep the peace or, worse still, to prevent acts of aggression and violence. Showing a willingness to discuss and negotiate can take away some of that need for control.

The empathic no

We're on safer territory here. The empathic no identifies with the desire and sees it for the marvellous thing it would be.

> 'I'd love to stay in bed all day too. It would be lovely. What films would we watch? We could watch them later when you get home from school.'

> 'I always get tempted to wear my new shoes on a muddy walk. They are lovely. They suit you.'

It can be a surprisingly successful approach. I guess that's because empathy shows our children that we are riddled with human frailty too and have many of the same urges and desires that they have. I admit that at first, I had to try quite hard to deploy the empathic no and then it became part of me and I realized that it's actually kindness and compassion. When we are locked into a domestic hellscape, kindness and compassion can get squeezed out.

Next-level empathy might be to recognize when our child has had enough and to then intervene: 'You look tired; shall we forget homework, get a takeaway and watch a film together?' Crumbs, they may think, you're actually quite nice.

The mind-reading no

When we are on top of our game, we will be able to anticipate a request before it lands on us and get in ahead of the question. This is a particularly useful strategy where there is a pattern to unreasonable requests and violent responses to hearing 'no'. Let's say that your loved one often asks you on a Thursday if they can stay out very late the following evening. This is what you might say perhaps on the Wednesday:

> 'On Thursdays, you sometimes ask me something that I can't say "yes" to. Shall we get it out of the way now?'

Or let's say that you've made an agreement that they can go out but you know from experience they are going to text you and ask for another hour. If you decline the request, you will be met with a torrent of abuse:

> 'We've agreed I will pick you up at 10. At some point, you're going to want to ask me to make that 11 or 12 and you'll want to change the pick-up point. I need you to know now that I won't agree to change our arrangement.'

The gobsmacked no

When a request isn't 'Can I have another biscuit?' or 'Can I wear my new slippers to school?' but more like 'Can I camp out for a few nights with my mates in my other mate's dad's field that's 30 miles away but I can't remember where it is? And can you take me and my mates there and stop off and get some booze on the way and lend me your phone because mine's crap?' there may be nothing for it but the gobsmacked no. It may not require too much faking, but it needs a modicum of humour.

> 'Are you having a laugh?'

> 'Nooooooo.'

> 'WHAT JUST HAPPENED?'

> 'Is this the dad of the mate of the mate who was arrested for beating the girlfriend of the uncle of the other mate?'

These are borderline sarcastic responses, if not closer than that, and sarcasm is a dangerous tool, but with older children, who if they had their way would not be parented at all, we have little left in our toolbox. Sarcasm can sometimes hit the mark, with minimal collateral damage. Using it is also quite enjoyable, especially when enjoyment is not something we experience very often. And let's face it, these situations we can find ourselves in are, in a dark way, really quite funny. They won't be what your parenting friends are dealing with, I'll bet.

When a 'no' really is a 'no'

As adults, we best serve our children by doing what is right and not what fear drives us to do. Our children may be keen to explore where 'no' is and keep driving at it. They may even get something out of challenging us and hearing the 'no' and may want the conflict. They may, however, also know deep down that we keep them safe, love them and care for them. They know that we must say 'no' and if we didn't, they wouldn't feel safe and their lives would be worse.

When to deliver a 'no'

If you really fear saying 'no' to something, if there is a risk that your child will react in an aggressive way, there are a few methods that you may want to try. We are in less than ideal territory here, and most parents never have to contend with these kinds of considerations.

As we've already discussed, buy yourself time and decide on the approach or approaches you are going to take. Be as regulated as you can. Consider holding the conversation when you are not alone. Consider where in the home to hold the conversation. Can you escape easily if things go wrong? Are the doors unlocked? Do you have access to your phone? You may prefer to be in a public place. You may choose to be in the car, if conversations in cars work for you. Could the 'no' be delivered by message or text? This distance can mean there is less heat in the conversation and some built-in thinking and regulating time. Have your safety plan in the front of your mind, just in case (see Chapter 8).

All of this extra thought and planning as well as dealing with any fallout takes an extraordinary amount of energy. You may feel wiped out after negotiating your way around a fiery child and a 'no' situation, and these situations may occur frequently. You must give yourself permission to recuperate and re-centre yourself. Without time for recovery, we are far less well equipped to deal with the next situation. And without wanting to be the bearer of too much bad news, when we begin using a few new techniques, our child may ratchet up their aggressive behaviour. In short, it might get worse before it gets better.

CHAPTER 8

What to Do in the Moment – The Red Zone

Carly

We're now going to think about what happens when actual aggression and/or violence is happening. How do we manage, what do we do, who do we call? It is enormously important to think about this stuff, even when it's not a regular occurrence. When we perceive aggression in any form, our brains and bodies move into a state of flight, fight or freeze, even if we appear to have more control over them in the moment. Think of that condescending or barbed passive aggressive remark that got sent firmly in your direction. You might well say nothing but feel quietly confused or hurt. You might laugh it off and think that the person is an idiot. You might talk it through with a friend, recounting what that person said to you through gently seething teeth. Whichever way you respond, your nervous system *will* get activated and mobilized towards flight or fight.

What does it look like when our children are in the Red Zone? Well, it ain't pretty. In terms of our nervous system states and capacity, we are talking about them operating from a place of *fight*. Their bodies are responding to a sense of *danger*, even if there is no actual danger present. Our children may be screaming and shouting at us (or someone else in the family), which could involve effing and jeffing, calling us every mother-trucking name that comes into their head. These words may be highly offensive and rejecting, and specific to what they know will hurt us most, not because they are necessarily thinking their insults through, but more because they are in survival mode and what comes out of their mouth is designed to make us back off or fill the terrifying metaphorical hole they have inside. For some children, especially older ones, their words may be combined with squaring up to us and yelling or screaming in our faces. They may be damaging (or attempting to damage) property or holding it aloft, threatening to do so with wide eyes, shallow, rapid breathing and every muscle tensed. They may be kicking, punching, biting, holding us down, hair-pulling or restricting our movement in any way, such as preventing us from leaving a room. It may be that their threats involve wielding weapons of some kind or even using them. Siblings and pets can be targets, too. For those on the receiving end or others present, it can be frightening and even if we 'remain calm', our own systems of survival will be activated.

As we have said before, Red Zone aggression is that mostly or fully out of control rage. It's not necessarily violent as it may be a verbal assault as opposed to physical violence or damage to property. Either way, it's full on and explosive. However, we also include 'menacing' anger or rage in the Red Zone. This is when a child is skulking, watchful, following us, invading personal space. It might also manifest as unkind comments snarled at us, condescending words or threats. Menacing rage feels as if the child/young person is in control and to a large extent they are, but they are very much *in* nervous system fight. Sometimes kids can remain in this state for days or weeks. It is edgy and claustrophobic to live with and reminds me of the iconic Alien 3 poster image of Sigourney Weaver, racked with sweat and wincing at the drooling face of the mother alien inches away from her own. Sigourney is waiting for her to strike. I remember one morning when Mr K was at work, my son was at school in Reception year and my two-year-old was home with me. Lisa, our foster daughter, was also at home (I forget why) and was in full-on menacing rage. At the time, she had a JD Bug scooter, which were very desirable items then. They came with a carry strap with two metal clips at either end so that you could easily carry your folded scooter over your shoulder (or over buggy handles in my case!). Lisa had been menacing all morning and I had tried to avoid conflict by going into a different room, sitting my two-year-old on my lap and reading her a story. I was followed in by my child in the Red Zone, who sat opposite me swinging the JD Bug strap with metal ends over her head, telling me that she could hit me in the head with it if she wanted. Menacing rage is that sort of thing. When you are in the throes of this type of aggression, some of the flight-safety and de-escalatory actions we looked at in the Amber Zone (Chapter 5) are also really helpful but the following Red Zone ideas also apply.

Out-of-the-blue aggression

I often get asked about 'random-and-out-of-the-blue' aggression. These are the little acts of violence that are seemingly unprovoked and catch us completely unawares and are usually most associated with younger children. A swift kick to the shin. A slap in the face. A hit on the arm. And we are left discombobulated because whatever was happening right before that was either nice or neutral. What's that about? I have some theories. In Chapter 4, we looked at why we have shame and how this gets socialized into guilt. Some of the children we are thinking about here have not had enough of their shame regulated early on and consequently they are easily triggered into it. When they are in the middle of play, young children often feel like masters of their own world; indeed, much of the process of imaginative play is called 'mastery' for that very reason. So, if a well-meaning parent who is playing with their child does something that is not within their child's projection of play, it can be felt as shame and the resulting manifestation of this might be to hit out. What we also know about trauma is that it creates negative internal working models (see Chapter 4) in children. These are internal models of ourselves, relationships and the world that get formed in early childhood. These children have models that say:

- I'm bad/worthless.

- Adults cannot/do not want to meet my needs (or are to be feared).

- The world is a difficult place that I must navigate to maintain safety.

For this reason, random acts of aggression can come when we are snuggled up on the sofa with our child or having a lovely time with them. Children suddenly become overwhelmed by the contrast between who they believe they are and what they believe they deserve and the love and fun we are having with them. This again can trigger shame or fear and before you know it, you've been clobbered. It sabotages a good moment for a child who doesn't believe they deserve it. The same effect can be true if that child perceives or hears a 'no'. Some children want physical affection and to be close to us but have not yet developed the trust or the means to seek this out in the usual ways. Instead of leaning into us, putting their arms out to us, koala-bearing our leg or asking for a hug, they dig an elbow in our side or slap our arm. There's also the problem that many of our children face where they have an extremely thin, barely perceptible 'line' between feeling excitement and feeling anxiety and fear. So, when excitement is felt, in a primal way this can also trigger an aggressive reaction. Of course, any actual anxiety can result in a seemingly random act of aggression if we haven't realized that our child is anxious.

How can we respond to a situation like this? When it happens, I invite parents to play catchphrase with their children and say what they see. Something like: 'Gosh, I wasn't expecting that... I'm not sure you were either... I wonder what made that happen... We need to work together to figure out what happens inside you when I get hit because I don't like getting hurt and my guess is that you don't like hurting me!' Being able to maintain calm and curious isn't easy after being hit but we can discharge a little of our own response with a surprised tone as opposed to attempting an ill-fitting whispery-oh-dear-me type of thing. It can help to keep a mental or physical memory of when 'random' aggression occurs as you may well spot a pattern.

When shit hits the fan (WSHTF)

When our children are in the Red Zone, we need to be damping down the fire, not pouring fuel on it. Stepping out of the ring, not inviting them into it. This isn't about showing fear or capitulation, rather an avoidance of entering the Red Zone ourselves because keeping our heads is vitally important. Some succinct phrases delivered firmly but without anger can help. Examples include:

- 'Okay, I'm backing off!'

- 'I'm making you angry, so I'm giving you space.'

- 'I need air!'

- 'I'm stepping outside.'

- 'Stop hitting!'

- 'I'm opening the door; please take a walk.'

WSHTF: Safety plan

We also need to keep our heads in order to implement the *safety plan*. This is an absolute essential when managing aggression and violence. The first time you experience a violent episode *or* when you feel aggression generally on the rise, you must devise a safety plan. This needs to include what, where, when and who:

What needs to happen if a violent episode occurs? What do you need to do? Leave the house? Call someone? If you are leaving the house, what do you need to take with you? Phone, car keys and any other family members (including pets) seem pretty essential. You may want to include purses and wallets if there is a risk money will be used for unhelpful means.

Where will you go? If your child/young person is receptive to talking about this stuff when they're in the Green Zone, you might also include somewhere *they* can go to if you and they have managed to achieve *them* leaving the house rather than you. You need to think of a nearby safe space, preferably the home of someone you trust, so you or your child can be safe and supported at the critical time.

When do you implement the plan? Where is your line, your boundary for seeking help and/or implementing the plan? This will be different in every single case. Perhaps it's when they start to damage items in the home or when they get right up in your face. You probably won't know where your line is until you've been through it a few times but once you do it's important that you stick to it. If you are co-parenting your child, both of you will need to agree when you implement the safety plan. So often I hear that one parent is saying that it's time to get outside help while the other wants to pursue managing their situation 'in house'. I think this sends a message to the child that the adults are out of their depth (which may well be true, but we avoid conveying this) and any sense of this can increase the child's fear (and therefore increase aggression).

Who do you involve? I think this is possibly the most important aspect of the plan. It may be that you must involve the police (more on this shortly) but you are more likely in the first instance to involve friends and family. Perhaps you send your other children to someone who lives nearby. You could also have a person or two on hand to call by the house if you call them or text them a word that means, 'Get your butt over here now, it's kicking off'. As with the 'where' aspect of your safety plan, you might need to arrange to get a key cut for someone's house in case you need to go there when no one is home. Whoever you involve, if that involvement means that they come face to face with your child as part of the plan, it needs to be someone who is not afraid of your child – preferably someone who will also love or care about your child despite what is happening and can convey that when the dust settles. This isn't such a key requirement if you are going to someone for refuge away from the aggression/ violence. There is, of course, a risk when we involve others that we convey to our child that they are bigger, scarier and more powerful than us and our love for them. Specifically, their perception is that *they* are more than we can handle when, in fact, it's their behaviour, of course. However, in this zone of aggression and violence, it needs to be safety first, and demonstrating to your children that you will take decisive action to maintain that is a good message. Also, the fact that you seek to re-engage and repair with your child after such an event is one of the most powerful therapeutic tools in your arsenal of love.

WSHTF: Holding

Sally once told me that she was reading a piece about a young woman who grew up in care who expressed her distress through violence and aggression. Here is what she said:

'I wish someone would have just f**king held me.'

This has resonance with my friend Sarah's comments in Chapter 3 when she recalled boundaries in foster care being a sign of safety and strength. So too, is the case when we stop our children hurting or damaging us, someone else or property. The shame and regret that they feel when their rage has been unleashed and left injuries and destruction in its wake is far greater than that which is curbed by holding. An example I often hear is when entire classrooms are evacuated when a child's behaviour has ventured into the realms of potential danger to others and the child continues to cause damage to the room. Sometimes, getting everybody out is the only option but leaving a child to continue to rage and damage isn't. Holding a child and removing them from that situation decreases their capacity to cause damage and reduces the resulting shame about returning to that room and those people later or the next day. In some ways, there may be a developmental element to holding our children if their early experiences have been traumatic and they did not have their rage regulated in toddlerhood. Many of us can recall picking up our two-year-old and removing them from a situation where they or another child might get hurt, or having to manhandle a dangerous object out of their grip that they've managed to swipe, or wrestling them into their car seat. All of these things were for their own or others' safety. They, of course, do not thank you for your interventions and they scream, fight and cry instead. But because of their relationship with you or the cuddle that happens soon after, episodes like this gradually decrease over time and they don't reach the age of ten and beyond fighting you when anything goes wrong. Their nervous system perceives whatever has gone wrong for what it is as opposed to threat and danger. Children who don't get to do toddler tantrums because they're too busy surviving don't get the chance to file a disappointment or inconvenience in the safe section of the brain's library, so responding to aggression/violence with holding potentially can fill those developmental gaps.

Team Teach is an organization that, among other things, teaches people how to safely hold children and young people. As part of their training, they tell us that any form of physical restraint of a person needs to be necessary, proportionate and reasonable. Of course, there is still a bandwidth of personal subjectivity when applying those three principles, isn't there? A child who is screaming obscenities at you with their face in yours may warrant the need to hold them. It also may not. Key to deciding whether to hold your child is the same as so many of the other options covered in this book. You know your child. You will have a sense of whether what they are presenting you with is likely to get you or someone else hurt, and, if it is not, you can ride it out in the other ways we've discussed.

If we reach the stage where we have had to hold our child, we want to do so for the least amount of time possible. The very best outcome of a hold is when the child moves through their fear-based response and can instead feel the deep sadness that is likely to be underneath their rage. And then they cry and allow your hold to turn into a long hug and the tone of your voice to regulate their shame. Moments like that are absolutely golden and I find that they also help us as the adults who have just lived through an episode of violence and holding to release a little of our own physical stress.

Holding children is controversial. It should be. We should never take it lightly and it's so important that we talk to others about needing to do this. People who are supporting you need to understand what you are living with and the lengths you are going to in order to keep everyone safe. It also helps to safeguard ourselves when, inevitably, your child marches into school the day after you have held them announcing that you have hurt them.

WSHTF: Calling the police

Anecdotally, families' experiences of involving the police around violence have been mixed, from utterly futile, to unhelpful, to amazing and supportive. Some parents are surprised when I start talking with them about involving the police in response to their child's violence. 'Can I do that?' one parent asked. Yep. Yes, you can. So, when? I suggest that calling the police can be done in two zones – in the emergency Red and in the reflective Green. Let's take the Red Zone first. If your child is too big for you to hold and their aggression or violence makes you fear for your own safety or if you are struggling to protect other family members, it's

probably wise to dial 999. You need help to get back to safety. When the
police arrive, depending on the scene they are met with, they may do a
lovely job of talking your child round to a calmer state. It might be that
their very presence diffuses the situation and usually they will ask you
if you feel safe for them to leave before they do so. It gets trickier when
they ask you what should happen next. Do you want to press charges?
Do you need the child to stay elsewhere and, if so, is there a family
member or friend who could have them stay over for an evening? Even
if events mean that the child is arrested, they'll most likely be released
within 24 hours and you will be asked if you, the victim, can have them
back home. This is also the kind of stuff you and your family are going
to need to think about when you devise your safety plan.

I have heard about a parent who has been informed that as a result
of violence towards her, which her son has been charged with, he'll be
court-directed to attend anger management sessions – which she'll have
to facilitate him going to but he won't go. And then what? He'll get a fine,
which his mother will need to pay, because he won't or he can't. So she,
the victim, has to pay for the perpetrator. To say that the criminal justice
and social care systems are ill-equipped to manage such situations is a
proverbial understatement. Having said that, I wouldn't want to detract
from those sensitive, intuitive police officers who do a wonderful job
of responding to these situations in the moment. In some cases, where
police are called out (often multiple times), they will leave your home
having assisted in regaining safety but will be sufficiently concerned as
to put a 'Treat as Urgent' (TAU) flag on your home so that any time you
call 999, the police recognize your home as being a priority in terms of
the need for them to respond.

Imagine now that you have had an episode of aggression or violence
and have managed to get through it without calling the police. Or perhaps there has been a general increase in aggressive behaviours, and you
have a sense that you might reach the point of needing to call the police.
I would encourage you while you are in a calm, Green space, to call
your local police and discuss your family situation with them. Ask what
would happen if you needed to call in an emergency. Get a sense of how
they support other families in the community with similar difficulties.
Sometimes both emergency and non-emergency contact with the police
can lead to one or two officers getting to know you and your child and
developing a helpful rapport. Having a sense of what might happen in

an emergency can help us feel more confident in the moment that we are doing the right thing.

Maintaining 'safe energy'

As I've already said, our bodies also become mobilized in the face of aggression (though it is also possible for us to demobilize into freeze). Sometimes we can use the mobilization in our body and voice to counter the child's rage. You could describe this as non-cowing but non-aggressive assertiveness; reserving the noise for when you really need it and harnessing the desire to lose your shit without doing it. When our nervous system gets mobilized, it needs mechanisms to demobilize or shake it off. The risk as parents/carers of being on the end of violence is that the stressful energy gets stored up in you. Cortisol can be corrosive and adrenaline can addle when they get stored up in our bodies. The other risk is that we end up discharging this on the child in an uncontrolled, enraged way. Training your body to dysregulate safely rather than denying your biological responses in the moment can be helpful.

Avoid eye contact

In direct contrast with the point above, sometimes we have to adopt a posture of non-threatening presence but to the point where we understand that any form of interaction will be perceived as a threat. This is not dissimilar to a freeze response, but it's more of an online, quietly mobilized freeze in which we simply engage as little as possible with our child. Much like the Bengal tiger example in the next chapter, it's about quietly existing around the rage. We do *not* recommend living like this for long. This way of being is for emergencies only and is not tenable, healthy or reasonable as a way of life – for anyone.

Their violence is our trauma

Our experience of living with aggression and violence is sometimes described as 'secondary trauma', that is, we begin to feel our children's trauma as if it were our own. It's a very real phenomenon and has a powerful impact on us. However, living with aggression and violence is *primary* trauma. There is nothing secondary about it. It's aimed at us, or our family members (or both), and we are having to use every fibre in our being to get through it, to survive. And that's before we do *any* of the stuff around us understanding what's going on for our child or attempting repair and reconnection or doing the scaffolding-behind-the-scenes to try to get our child being and feeling safer.

Here's an example of the difference between secondary and primary trauma in terms of how it impacts on us. When we were fostering, one morning I woke up, went through the daily routine of making coffee, packed lunches, saying goodbye with a hug to our foster daughter as she left for school, and walking the tiddlers to school. This was a day when, having taken them to school, I returned home rather than going for a run. Mr K was also home. I became aware of a deep sense of sadness and realized I'd been feeling that way for a couple of days. When I shared this with Mr K, he replied, 'Weird! Me too!' And then, as if we were in a film, we paused, looked at each other and said, 'Lisa'. We both twigged that her sadness, which wasn't massively evident, but she was hiding well, had become ours. That was secondary trauma. Another time we were going through an extremely difficult patch with Lisa that included bouts of aggression. One morning, after a particularly spikey and loaded exchange, she left for school slamming the door so the whole house rattled. Poor old Mr K then proceeded to go upstairs and vomit. That was primary trauma – his reaction to living with negotiating threat and aggression over a few weeks. Chapter 13 will talk more about how this stuff impacts us but, in the meantime, be aware that when responding to Red Zone situations, we ourselves will *at least* be in the Amber Zone and need the foresight of thinking through these strategies ahead of time to give us the best chance of making it through the Red Zone.

CHAPTER 9

The Psychology of Trauma

—— Carly ——

In Chapter 4, we looked at the neurological and biological legacy of trauma and we'd like to extend this by considering how it affects the way children make sense of themselves, relationships and the family atmosphere because, as we've previously said, seeking to understand how our child perceives the world is a helpful tool in our peace-keeping, empathy-maintaining arsenal. Several years ago, one of my dearest friends was killed in a road traffic accident. As you can imagine, it was sudden and unforeseen and those who loved her were, of course, grief stricken. I remember after a few days entering a phase where I felt utterly alone, and I was angry to be alone. In fact, there was nothing further from the truth. I was, and still am, a loved person with a caring family and some utterly stonkingly brilliant friends. I could have called on any of these people who would have been straight over and happy to hold me while I bawled my eyes out and left snot all over their shoulder. What stopped me doing that wasn't anything to do with how things were, it was to do with how I felt and thought things were. My sadness at the loss of this one, beautiful friend was so deep that for a few days I felt as if I didn't have any other friends. This experience was a visceral taste of how it can feel for children who view the world, relationships and even themselves as unsafe. It is incredibly difficult to 'convince' someone that they are safe when they don't feel it.

Mission control

It follows that in a world where being able to stay emotionally and physically safe is a state to grasp and cling onto rather than a given, one would be organized by achieving this. We know that children with a disorganized attachment style display controlling behaviours and this is because they have experienced some degree of abusive parenting. It therefore follows that, from their point of view, being in control helps them to minimize the risk of this happening again. But it's not only developmental trauma that makes children feel the need for control. Issues such as parental separation, bereavement, intrusive medical intervention and experiences of racism can all leave children feeling vulnerable and as if life is being done to them rather than being an interactive participant in it. When that happens, a normal and proportionate response is to tighten their grip on aspects of their lives that they can control, like what they eat or who they hang out with or which route they walk to school or how many times they turn a light on and off before going to bed. If other people thwart or try to prevent those attempts at control, it can feel unsafe and result in outbursts on the spectrum of violence. As Brene Brown puts it, when we turn to self-protection, we 'choose' 'certainty over curiosity, armour over vulnerability and knowing over learning'.[4]

TIP

When our children insist on doing something that we strongly sense is a bad idea that will lead to a bad outcome but attempting to stop them outright will lead to aggression, a helpful phrase to use, with directness about our eye contact and strength in our tone of voice is, 'I DO NOT think that is a good idea, but I'm not going to stop you!'

Yet another reason for control

The impact of the Covid-19 pandemic and its lockdowns caused ripples in our need for more control. Tickets for flights, theatre, gigs, football matches got cancelled over and over again by something that didn't have a face. We wanted to see friends and family when we could not. Would children go to school, or wouldn't they? Would they be doing exams, or not? That general sense of safety we all have in the predictability of life was shattered. Even the removal of the mundane and boring aspects of life was desta-bilizing. Most people would agree that the pandemic had (and is still having) a significant impact on mental health in general but I think it highlighted our collective and individual human reliance on predictability. When our life patterns become unpredictable, our internal need to control increases.

Do my anger for me

Until I started to foster, I didn't know I had so much anger inside myself. To be clear, that doesn't mean I was screaming and shouting at my kids, it means I just felt it much more acutely than I ever had before. I found myself wondering where it all came from and realized that it wasn't all mine, it was my foster daughter's. I began describing it as if my little bit of anger would get a resonant frequency with her big bit of anger. That glare she sent my way or that door slam or the comment she made about me to my friend would make my anger flare up. I believe that what was happening does so a great deal in families where trauma is a factor and I've had multiple conversations about this with parents who describe how their child can explode a metaphorical bomb in someone else in the family. It's a way of doing their anger by proxy. It's when they say or do something, usually minor, and feel a sense of satiation that someone is doing their anger for them. Sometimes this is completely subconscious, other times it's deliberate. When we as parents are pushed into exploding ourselves, this can actually regulate our child. Our child seeing and feeling the other's dysregulation regulates their own. I am not suggesting explosive parenting to 'help' with a child's dysregulation because it brings out the worst in us and doesn't work at all in the long run. I certainly never felt like a good person or parent when that happened.

Over the years, whether at home or in a therapy session, I have often used the 'playing Catchphrase' technique when I can see a child trying to 'poke' a family member for a reaction. I'd say something like:

'Darling, it feels as though you're trying to give me your big feelings/some of your anger right now. I'd rather not take it but I'm happy to try to help you with it.'

'Ah! I noticed you called your Mummy those words! It feels as if maybe you're cross about this conversation, and you want to make Mummy cross instead?'

'You usually do/say [insert relevant behaviour] when you need me to notice that you're worried/upset/cross about something. Can I guess what might be worrying you?'

You can also do this in a more energized, fast-paced way that can be more helpful with older children. Something like:

'You're trying to make me own your feelings. They are yours but I'm here to help.'

'I think you're trying to get me to explode. I'm not up for that but I do want to help.'

Dysregulation imported

For the children we are thinking about, home is most likely to be their safe space and the violence they enact is about other stuff, some of which is so common we have written about it individually later. School and social media are two giants in triggering utter emotional mayhem in our children, which translates into a shitshow at home. Not fun. If I'm really honest, I don't think I can imagine what it takes to get through a day, especially a school day, if you are a traumatized child or young person. Perhaps it's akin to running up hill in blistering heat while having to look out for morsels of food and water which you must grab and consume as you continue running. Or maybe treading shark-containing water all day while memorizing the dictionary. Or solving maths equations in the same room as a Bengal tiger. Our children are trying to manage rules, relationships, rooms, smells, periods, parties, food, sensory needs, TikTok, tests and it's *Very. Hard. Work.* And how each of our children navigates that stuff will be different. Since we've mentioned Bengal tigers, the very reason that came to mind was because I've used the following metaphor numerous times in my work with young people who engage in risky behaviours. I say to the young person:

'Imagine there was a Bengal tiger in this room right now. Here's how I'd respond. I would immediately start praying that the tiger would not eat me. I'd stay still, avoid eye contact and also pray that it would enjoy the feel of my rug, settle down and fall asleep. Then, if it did, I'd slowly and extremely carefully get up and attempt to sneak out of the room. You, however, would respond by trying to pull out the tiger's whiskers.'

Young people fully understand the point I'm making: that their response to danger is often dangerous or, in the case of teachers, plain unhelpful. It is, of course, not the young person's fault. In the case of a pattern of abusive, frightening early life, it makes absolute sense, but my comments are about increasing self-awareness because when it comes to helping children with aggression, self-awareness is important. They need help to understand their bodies and the corresponding feelings. Many of our children's responses to how they manage their trauma in the world are seen in all their tricky glory at home.

Re-creation of early life

Some children's abusive early experiences get played out in the here-and-now in their loving families. Children who are exposed to drug/alcohol/abuse or extreme stress in-utero and children who have lived through domestic violence generally have a monumentally compro-mised capacity for regulation *and* a high drama drive, both of which can be expedients for children becoming violent later in life. Epigenetic studies (the study of heritable changes in gene activity that are not due to the DNA sequence) have shown[5] that foetuses exposed to trauma in the 911 attacks in New York, like their mothers, had reduced levels of cortisol in their saliva which is a key hormone relating to regulation.

These children's demands for material possessions, drugs, alcohol or risky experiences can lead to us as parents having to say no to those demands and we all know what 'no' can result in. Many children I have worked with who lived in those high-octane environments with strangers coming and going, violence, noise and chaos seem to need some of that long after they have been removed from those homes. For children unfortunate enough to have had multiple family moves, that can reinforce the exposure to instability.

As we said earlier, many children struggle to cope with quiet because their own thoughts are intrusive and difficult. Calm feels alien and the need to create drama, which feels familiar, is essential. Adopted and fostered children and young people often attempt, in an unconscious way, to re-create the drama of their early environment. This is drama which is sometimes perpetuated in a different way by the fostering and adoption process itself: multiple carers, multiple social workers, contact with their birth family, multiple adults visiting and asking them questions, adults having conversations about them. When something has been a way of life in your most formative years, sometimes you just feel safer with the devil you know.

TIP

Wonder with your child about why quiet is hard.

The other aspect of this goes back to our bread-and-butter knowledge around attachment. If you have an attachment style which includes the idea that you can't rely on others or that others will ultimately let you down, you tend, again unconsciously, to do a couple of things. One: you surround yourself with relationships that confirm this world view so that you get to tell yourself 'told you so'. You might hang out with the selfish types that use and abuse you or engage in high-drama activities. Two: you hang out with people who aren't like this but the way you interact with them causes them to behave more like the ones who are. For example, if I have an ambivalent attachment, I might be prone to attaching very quickly to new friends. I then might be in contact with them a lot because I feel that out of sight (or text or message or social media) might also be out of mind. I start interpreting their 'slow' or brief responses as disinterest or rejection so I might become more demanding of them or give them the cold shoulder in response. This could then actually make them start to feel that this is a relationship they need to have more distance from, thus fulfilling my view that people are unreliable and cannot be trusted and I am not good enough to be a part of their life.

Relationships = Drama

Testing and trust

When I'm training parents, carers and various professionals about the inner world of the traumatized child, I always include this concept: when we're a child, we never expect to move home or lose our parents;

until that happens. Then we *always* expect it, from an ever-looming sense in our bones to a mild whisper from one or two cells in our body. Wherever we are on that spectrum, we believe we are not worthy of permanence and unconditional parental love. For this reason, children become consciously and unconsciously suspicious when things are going really well or when they have gone really wrong.

In the case of the former, where daring to trust an adult is brave, children question why life and their relationship with their parent/carer feels so positive, so reciprocal, because this is a feeling they're not used to. Surely, they don't deserve this, or the parents/carers will notice any time soon that they are actually bad and not entitled to this happiness. Children's aggression usually comes from fear and in this case, it is fear of rejection. It's not premeditated or thought through, it's reactive fear when something has gone wrong, and they are afraid you've discovered that they really are a terrible human: 'If I can push you to scream at me, I will prove I'm the hideous child I believe myself to be.'

Children fear losing us yet do not believe they deserve us. It's like when warm, humid air collides with cold dry air, and you get a tornado. It's so confusing. So, the child finds themselves doing something outrageous, like stealing, hiding poo or getting *very* easily triggered into aggression and violence. They orchestrate rejection to have some semblance of control over what they believe is the inevitable but that is scary and makes their capacity extremely low and ready to leap into a state of fight. In the case when something has gone wrong, there may have been a rupture in the child-parent/carer relationship, or the child might be anticipating this because of whatever has happened. They feel intense and pervasive shame.

Dan Hughes[6], founder of the dyadic developmental psychotherapy approach teaches us that there are several reactions a child has to shame-inducing incidents. They are: deny the incident, minimize it, blame someone for it, go into rage. You don't need to be a genius to realize that these responses occur when the child is mobilized and therefore in flight or fight.

PART 3

Develop Strategies and Create an Environment for Reflection and Repair

CHAPTER 10

Why Therapeutic Parenting?

Carly

I think it's fair to say that trauma in all its guises brings with it some form of damage, a word I am using carefully. Whether it's the absence of emotional connection, the loss of someone we love, a seismic shift in the world we thought we knew or abusive experiences, trauma puts us on our guards. If ever we knew what it was like to live relatively carefree and safe, or whether it was tough from before we were born, trauma forces us to focus a little/a lot more on survival than 'thrival'. You have probably picked up by now that the changes that trauma brings in our children demand changes in us as parents. Therapeutic parenting is about adapting our children's physical and emotional environment, so they have a better chance of living closer to the 'thrival' end of the spectrum. We don't expect babies to use toilets or wheelchair users to use stairs. Nappies and ramps are celebrated items that enable full potential, be it now or later in life. In the same way, Sally and I have found that therapeutic parenting, rather than making excuses for children, is enabling their trust and emotional regulation to grow in the context of their relationship with carers/parents and other important adults.

Therapeutic parenting starts with the child and seeing the world through their eyes. A therapeutic parent looks out for opportunities to *go to* their child rather than expecting the child to *come to them* (in a physical and emotional sense) and they look out for tiny clues about what's happening in their child's internal and external world so they can be with their child for it or do something that might help or let the child know that they're enjoying something by the big smile on their face.

Many traumatized children struggle to read the world so therapeutic parenting must interpret it for them until they can.

Emotional environment

When you live with a child who displays violent or aggressive behaviour it can feel as if the trauma is personified by an invisible entity of its own, like an angry dog or a small monster that you haven't invited to live with you but there they are. Sometimes that can be helpful because when you're up against it, feeling angry and hurt (which is normal and acceptable), it can feel less personal and hurtful that it comes from invisible dogs and monsters than your child. The difficulty is that these trauma characters can start to affect the tone or the atmosphere of family life negatively. You start to feel that:

- you are organized by them

- you're acquiescing to their every whim

- your own life is being constricted by them

- your family life is being constricted by them

- it's hard to feel joy

- you are stagnant.

Essentially, the dogs and monsters set the tone of the family atmosphere rather than the adults. Therapeutic parenting is aware of this risk and looks out for it. Many of the Green Zone techniques feed into how we monitor family atmosphere and respond when it starts to go askew, or as my Granny used to say, skew-whiff.

Strongly related to this is the creation of an environment that allows children to grow into who they are. We use the garden metaphor because gardens need cultivating. My garden needs a particular type of grass seed because the soil is so hideously cloggy. Some plants need cutting back after they bloom. Others need leaving. Some need various sized sticks to guide them in the right direction. Therapeutic parenting is like that but instead of soil, cutting and sticks, it creates opportunities for success, avoids failure and puts the relationship first, providing choices and consequences, and showing how we do sorry, acceptance and empathy.

Creating success and avoiding failure

This looks entirely different for each child but it's mostly about setting small, achievable goals, quitting while you're ahead and promoting what they're ready for. This might be organizing a playdate that you structure well and keep brief or leaving a party early before a 'meltdown' occurs. If they get a mobile phone, it could mean restricting their number of apps or limiting when they can have it. Or introducing them to a new school in a slow and planned way. It might involve brave decisions around school, like one family who decided that certain GCSEs could not be passed by their child and pulled them out of those, relieving pressure on their child and allowing them to focus on the ones they could achieve.

Putting the relationships first

Delivered in the wrong way, this looks like being mates with your child or letting them do or have what they want. That might be fine when they are firmly an adult in chronological and emotional terms, but while they are a child, they need parents. The idea of putting the relationship with your child first is more of an overarching philosophy about valuing the relationship with your child over aspects of raising them that you know are good for them, for example binning off reading with our foster daughter as described in Chapter 3 or letting them go to that party that you know might end in tears or letting them open all their Christmas presents on 1st December. It is very much a long game. Just occasionally, the world teaches our children the lessons we want them to learn. That's not to say that that we won't have to deal with some or all of the fallout, but they might think twice before making fake or secret social media accounts and using their actual phone number as their username or giving up learning to play an instrument or hanging out in *that* part of town at night.

Choices and consequences

The world we live in is a highly evaluative one. How this makes each of us feel varies between highly motivating and helpful, extremely anxiety provoking, utterly indifferent, butterflies-in-stomach-inducing and massively megalomaniacal. In therapeutic parenting, there is an emphasis on choices and 'natural' consequences as opposed to rewards and sanctions.

Children with a poor view of themselves expect to fail or to get it wrong so the likes of sanctions if they do are not motivating factors for a change in behaviour because they do *not* change how children/young people feel about themselves, relationships or the world. Similarly, behaving for rewards or even getting those rewards doesn't change how they feel. When we apply rewards and sanctions there is often an undertone of:

> That makes me happy: 'You saved your chocolate/your pocket money, good girl!'

Or,

> That's made me cross: 'You ate all your chocolate/spent all your pocket money at once and now you want more! Maybe next time you won't be so silly!'

What therapeutic parenting aims for in choices and consequences is for the child to change how they feel about themselves and link *their* feelings to their actions:

> 'I'm glad that you're happy with your choice.'

And,

> 'I'm sorry you're unhappy with your choice.'

Or,

> 'I noticed how pleased you were when you saved your pocket money for that t-shirt. Good for you!'

And,

> 'I'm sorry you're left without any pocket money this weekend. You look disappointed that you've spent it.'

When children and young people's behaviour is unacceptable, much like the examples given above, there will be a very natural consequence for this, such as no money or chocolate at the weekend because they've already used it up, but sometimes, we as parents need to implement those consequences. When doing so we still seek to relate them to what happened.

Sometimes the consequences are even environmental. Years ago, I realized that our foster daughter had been stealing money from a piggy bank on the shelf and it was clear that the money had been spent on junk and sugary food. Mr K and I talked about how to manage it and realized that leaving the money 'available' where it was had been an oversight on our part and consequentially, we would not leave money 'out' like that again. We found a way to 'talk' about this with Lisa which I'll discuss in the next part on how we do sorry. Some times the best consequence is: 'We need to talk about this.'

I assure you, talking about it is one of the more difficult consequences from our children's point of view. What about violence? What consequences are helpful when stuff gets broken, or someone gets hurt? Some of this will be covered in Chapter 14 but two invaluable principles to hold on to are *connection before correction*[7] and *striking while the iron is cold*. The first refers to the need to emotionally connect with your child with empathy and acceptance (see later) before we repair and manage consequences. It's about letting the child know that you still care for them and want them in your life, that you and they are 'all right'. It might be happening after they've run to their room and holed themselves up, after you've had to hold/restrain them, after you've called the police or got round someone on your safety plan, or they have stayed out all night with goodness-knows-who doing you-don't-know-what or after you have utterly messed up because of your Amber or Red Zone responses to a straw that broke the sodding camel's back, or even after them being arrested.

Whatever you and they have been through, connection can happen through notes under the door, texts, face-to-face chats, phone calls or holding each other in a messy, bawling snotty heap on the kitchen floor. One family I worked with sellotaped crisps to notes they were posting under the bathroom floor when their foster son locked himself in there, saying they were worried that he hadn't eaten in a long time and it was the only food that would fit under the door! Sometimes we have enough levity in us to do that. Other times we do not. As Sally says in Chapter 14, sometimes it's just a quick 'in and out' – 'I'm here, it will be okay and we'll sort this' – until such a time as we can muster something more than that.

Striking while the iron is cold refers to the timing of this connection and correction. It's about connecting and repairing when the child is back in the Green Zone or at least on the Green side of Amber. If we go in too soon with, 'What happened just then wasn't okay...' or, 'I'm really sad to see you feeling so upset', or, 'We need to talk about how to make this right', we risk sending them back/further into the fight state we so carefully navigated them away from.

For some children, striking while the iron is cold means hours or days later and, as has already been said, the *mode* of communication can make all the difference to when they are ready to hear what you have to say. Sometimes we can feel as though boundaries are violated again and again. As several families have put it to me, 'We just have no control over anything they're doing any more'. Most of us have heard the philosophical thought experiment, 'If a tree falls in the woods and no one is around to hear it, does it make a sound?' It is a bit like that with boundaries. Just because a child crosses a boundary doesn't mean they don't exist. It's painful, frustrating and depressing when that happens but that doesn't mean you agree with what's happening. Safety boundaries still stand and are still important and you can still live by them.

Praise

What about when children's behaviour *is* acceptable or kind or regulated or they make that positive choice? Praise is perfectly possible but the delivery of it is important because if we make it too big or gushing it will loudly and clearly clash with their internal brittle voice of badness and could trigger aggression or violence. For children where this is apt, praise should be quiet or under the radar and try to focus on your experience of being with them or your experience of their achievements and behaviours, such as:

'I had a fun time with you this afternoon.'

'I enjoyed our day today.'

'Thank you for showing me your picture; it was good to see it.'

'Thank you for your help in taking the dog for a walk.'

'I think you tried hard today.'

'I noticed you looked out for your friend today. I thought that was kind.'

'I thought you speaking to our new friend today was brave.'

'I noticed you brushed your teeth this morning without me asking you. I hope you didn't miss my nagging!' (playful)

This way of conveying praise or even love in small ways slowly, slowly helps the child see them through our eyes and it cannot be rushed. Other ways of doing this are notes in lunchboxes that say 'Thinking of you! ♥ Mum' or 'Enjoy your lunch! Xxx' are lovely. Also 'knowing' winks or little kisses on top of their heads as you walk past or a light touch or their shoulder or back can say so much without them feeling exposed or overwhelmed. When our foster daughter Lisa had her first birthday with us, we had got to know her well enough that we planned it carefully around her struggle to accept love, praise and positivity. Together we planned that our family would go to her favourite place to eat, Pizza Hut (other pizza restaurants are available), with her best friend's family. Lisa said that she would like a cake but not candles or singing. As a parent, that goes against a lot of what we want for our children, but time had taught us that she was right – doing that would probably be too much. When we got home, Lisa, Lauren and our birth son were straight out in the street to play on their scooters (Lisa had a new one for her birthday that morning) and the adults hung around chatting and making sure the kids didn't get hit by a car. I waited until Lisa was sat on our wall and then I got the cake. I quietly got down low beside her and whisper-sang 'Happy Birthday' with the cake (we had briefed our friends on how low key it all needed to be, so they took no notice). I smiled at her, and she smiled at me before I went inside, cut the cake and brought bits out on kitchen roll (classy, I know) and handed them out. End. Of. Birthday. But I know she was able to feel loved that day without it activating that awful feeling inside that she didn't deserve any of it. If your child has that unworthy, unlovable sense of self, when it comes to praise and conveying our love, a subtle, measured approach is therapeutic.

Saying sorry

Therapeutic parenting recognizes that shame prevents children saying sorry, at least for a while, because shame says that *they* are the bad, rather than the choice/behaviour is bad. As we've seen earlier, shame is the rocket-fuel trigger for aggression and violence. I should emphasize that where children have had a positive start in life and have experienced relational safety, this may not apply and saying sorry might not be so difficult, though likely still a challenge if control is important to them. We all like to hear children say sorry (and mean it) when they do things wrong, and some adults expect it. Children understand this and sometimes 'learn' to say sorry, frankly to get adults off their back or make them happy. I have known many children who have become angry when their 'apology' is questioned or not accepted because they have followed the rules of societal acceptance. 'BUT I SAAAAAAID SORRYYYYY!' they yell. They come to think it is a get out for talking about the issue any further. This is a particularly difficult one as a parent, because even if we decide not to insist on apologies from our children, other people will. Helping children reach a point where, as one parent helpfully puts it, they *own* their behaviour, can in be done in stages.

Sorry for

This acknowledges that the child will not be able to say a meaningful sorry due to shame or still being angry. Where an apology is needed, especially where others have been hurt or affected by our child's behaviour, we might need to do this for them. That might sound like:

> 'I'm sorry you got hurt/I'm sorry your toy got broken. That shouldn't have happened and I'm really sorry it did. It wasn't okay for Rosie to do that.'

When our child is more regulated and able to reflect, we might let them know that we've made this repair, particularly if it's in the context of talking with the child about what went wrong:

> 'I let Lauren know that you were sorry for hitting her/breaking her toy.'

That way a child knows that a sorry is necessary but doesn't have to worry as much about facing the child and having to do this themselves. That might sound like an enormous cop-out for the child and as if we're setting them up for never having to say sorry, but in the context of a therapeutic parenting approach, it helps a child move towards being able to do this for themselves. We do it for toddlers all the time because we accept that they don't have the verbal skills or the social capacity to do this when they snatch a toy or break something. Instead, we model it and do sorry for them, in front of them. When I needed to address Lisa stealing money from that piggy bank, I knew it would massively dysregulate her and could have turned violent. I thought long and hard about the best way of doing this. At the time, Lisa had an established evening routine involving lots of nurture and part of that was me brushing her wet hair after she'd had a bath. I would sit on the sofa and she would sit in front of me on the floor while she watched TV and I brushed. I chose this time to talk to her because she didn't have to look at me (therefore less shame and confrontation), there was the distraction of the TV (decreasing the intensity of the conversation) and there was a mobilized but calm activity happening (hair brushing). I said to her:

> 'I need to say sorry to you for something. I have realized that money has been going missing from the piggy bank on the bookshelf and it wasn't fair of me to leave money around like that. I know it's so hard when money is around because you like it to buy sweets and biscuits to make the stress of school easier. It's also really hard for you to ask for money so if it's left out, you take it. So, I'm sorry I put the money where you'd be tempted to take it and I want to let you know that we won't do that again.'

I had to address her behaviour, and in this case, I decided that talking about it was enough. I could have set up reduced pocket money over several weeks to pay it back but on this occasion it didn't feel necessary. The fact that I was able to talk to her about it without her dysregulating and still getting a hug before bed was enough to convince me that it was the right call.

Sorry with

Once there is enough safety in our relationship with a child, we can move on to 'doing sorry' with them. We may still need to say 'sorry for' in the first instance; where others have been hurt, they may need to hear 'sorry' from someone but it's likely we will need to give the child who has hurt them more time. They will be in the Amber or Red Zones for a while and they can only do meaningful sorries when they're in the Green Zone. This kind of sorry is a scaffolded one. When we are talking with our child about what has gone wrong, we can introduce the concept of saying sorry or making a repair.

'I know you had a really tricky afternoon. Let's have a hot chocolate and we can think about how we can make things right with Rosie because it wasn't okay that she got hurt.'

Or:

'Tomorrow you'll stay off school because I think you need some breathing space. I will also need to talk to Mr Bower about paying for the broken glass and what you will need to contribute. He's not angry but I think we should find a way to say sorry to him, too.'

This does not have to be a face-to-face sorry. It can be written or emailed, it could be buying a gift as a sorry or doing an act of sorry, such as:

'I think we need to do something for Dad because it wasn't nice for him to get called a f**king w**ker. Shall we make him a cup of tea and biscuits?'

The magic happens the most where those receiving the sorry can do so with grace. This might mean that the (act of) sorry is delayed until the injured party is in their Green Zone. If a child attempts a sorry only to be met with 'well, that's not good enough' or is given the silent treatment, this will undo the work you are trying to do with them. They need an experience of their apology being accepted before they can move on to doing it for themselves.

Owning sorry

I work with a family for whom the word 'sorry' unfortunately got wrapped up in a bundle of hideous abuse in their first family and, along with the extreme levels of shame that it left the children with, meant that the meaning of the word got befouled. Instead, when something goes wrong, the children are invited to 'own it'. I like this a great deal because it sends a message to the child that even if they do not own it, it still happened and requires a response of some sort. For example, if a child breaks something of yours, you will still need to replace it, which will cost you time and money. A natural consequence of that is that you might have less time to spend in the park that day and less money to buy their usual ice-cream or treat.

As with doing sorry with a child, when they get to the point of being able to do it for themselves, the receivers of the sorry, where possible, need to accept it. That will, of course be harder where children are involved. Sadly, it can reach the point where children or siblings have been hurt or had their class disrupted so many times that they are no longer willing to accept a sorry, which we need to respect. We can only compassionately talk about this with our child as a natural consequence of their aggression. There are times when a child is attempting a sorry but they're not entirely aware they are doing so. I often hear parents say, 'I knew he felt bad because he offered to make me a drink' or, 'I knew she was sorry because she tidied her room, which is what I asked her to do in the first place!' When we notice a child attempting a sorry it can be helpful for us to make them aware, for example, when they bring you the cup of tea you might say, 'Oh, thank you. I think this feels a bit like you saying sorry. I appreciate that' or when they've tidied something, 'This looks great! It's as if your room has said sorry for you, thank you' (not with sarcasm but warmth) or, 'This feels like a sorry cuddle. I like it, thank you.'

Acceptance

When one is living with violence, one of the worst aspects is not knowing what to do. There is a sense of wanting to make it all stop and fix whatever it is about your child that is making them do this. When we hear the word 'acceptance' in the context of violence it can feel jarring or even offensive or woolly, like 'letting yourself be a doormat parent'. It isn't woolly because it's like creating a highly reflective map of your child that you return to again and again, making alterations the more they grow and the more you learn about them. It fundamentally provides *emotional context* for whatever has gone wrong. What I think is a bit magical about acceptance is that it opens doors for our children to tell us a bit more because it doesn't invalidate feelings. It might start small, with our child telling us, 'I'm rubbish at maths.' If we respond with acceptance, 'Oh, you feel as if you're rubbish at maths? That sounds hard for you,' they may tell us the following week that they find the peer they sit next to in maths scary. If we respond more traditionally, 'Oh no, darling, you're good at maths. You got four out of five on your test last week', then we may never get to hear that they're afraid of the child they sit next to. And if we don't know about that then we can't do anything about it and, arguably more importantly, we can't move into empathy. We can't 'stay' with that fear and how hard it is for them.

Dan's Two Hands Theory

It's difficult for me to talk about acceptance without citing Dan Hughes' Two Hands Theory[8] so I won't try. Dan talks about how we, as parents and adults must judge behaviour. In fact, most countries have a system of judging behaviour of adults by other adults, so it's universal. According to Dan, when it comes to our children, it's all the other stuff behind the behaviour that we don't judge and instead, accept, such as:

Thoughts: I don't think I'll get enough to eat today.

Feelings: That kid in school scares me.

Beliefs: Mum loves my brother more than me.

Motives: I need to try to not get in trouble at school.

Perspective: I'm a bad person.

Experience: Abusive parenting, multiple carers.

When applied to therapeutic parenting, this helps a child to make sense of whatever has happened far more meaningfully and gives them a chance to avoid shame (or, at least, make it less potent). We are encouraged to name those thoughts, feelings, beliefs and so on with the child and accept them because they can't just switch them off and it takes (a long) time for them to change (of course, historical experience does change but new ones can be introduced). Two Hands is about accepting all the 'other' stuff with one hand and addressing behaviours with the other. We can therefore better understand the 'why' behind a behaviour and help our child understand it too. More importantly, it (sometimes) boosts our empathy for when it goes wrong. When my child walked off the school playing field, red faced and yelling at their games teacher that he was a 'f**king goon', it was triggering as a parent. Yet if I know and accept that she feels afraid at school, feels terrified about being singled out, believes that she is bad, has experienced fear-based punishment, and perceived that the teacher was expressing a dislike for her, I'm able to make sense of what happened and help her make sense of it too. We still need to find a way to repair for the behaviour (covered in the rest of this chapter) but in the meantime, acceptance can reduce the enormous shame she is feeling about it. The truth is that I didn't initially respond to this incident with my foster daughter with a huge amount of acceptance. I was still getting my head around therapeutic parenting, but we did repair and some extremely helpful school-based tweaks were put in place after that because certain members of staff were also interested in acceptance (see Chapter 18).

Empathy

I must confess that I don't think that, for British people, empathy is their first language. Or second or third. It's not our fault, it is the way we were raised, and living through one or two World Wars rather inspires a 'mustn't-feel-the-pain-must keep-going' spirit of survival. According to Brene Brown, 'empathy is a brave choice' because it means us feeling some of the pain that others are feeling and therefore connecting with whatever feeling we have that resonates with theirs. Empathy is about staying with whatever our children feel, naming it, being with it. Our children often feel as though they shouldn't be feeling as they do – sad, angry, excited, confused, afraid. So, when we give them empathy, it normalizes those feelings or validates them. If we fall into trying to fix their pain or anger or tell them 'it will be fine' or 'you shouldn't feel that way' then they either decide they shouldn't tell us how they feel again, or it plays into the hands of them feeling that their feelings are wrong – that they shouldn't be there.

Empathy gives us the opportunity to allow our children to feel 'big feelings' at a deeper level as they sense *us* feeling them with them without becoming overwhelmed. It makes sense that children who are aggressive or violent get that way through an overload of emotions. Not only does empathy convey to the child that their feelings make sense, but it also does so in the context of their relationship with you. Whatever their model of relationships until this point, empathy may be a new and revelatory experience for your child and therefore assists in 'dragging them into consciousness' (see Chapter 5) in a powerfully connecting way. In my work, one way I describe conveying empathy is 'staying with the shit'. While a tad crude, it does serve for the most part to get to the point. If I say to you, 'My child is frequently violent towards me', and you say, 'Okay, have you tried grounding them' or, 'I just think you need to not take any of their crap. I wouldn't be treated that way', I will feel unheard, judged, like a rubbish parent and that you think I am stupid. However, if you respond to that same statement with, 'Oh wow, I had no idea, I'm so sorry; that sounds awful' or, 'Oh my gosh, I'm not really sure what to say but I'm really glad you told me... Can I help in any way?'

I will breathe a sigh of relief and feel that my pain has been heard and I can continue to tell my story. And isn't that the place that we want our children to get to? For them to feel able to tell us what they are feeling and what is happening for them. To get to the heart of 'why' our child is violent, we need them to be able to talk to us, but they cannot do that without a therapeutic approach that raises their internal awareness, verbalizes that to us and encourages more of that by us staying *with* those feelings. It is not about being avoidant of them or appalled, dysregulated or disgusted by them. When our child has sworn at a teacher, hit their sibling, taken a peer's toy from their bag or smashed something up, acceptance first seeks out the feelings behind that behaviour:

'Wow, that teacher must have said something to really upset you!'

'Okay, I can see you were so angry with your brother!'

'You had soooo many worries today. So much worry.'

'Oh love, you were so upset that your Mum/Dad didn't come to see you today.'

Empathy stays with it for long enough to let the child know that you can handle those feelings, that they are understandable and that you care enough to be alongside them in those feelings:

'You were so scared when your teacher asked you to share your family tree... You didn't know what to say. You didn't know how to talk about all your brothers and sisters and us too. It was too hard, and you were so worried about what the other children would think.'

'I know that you find it sooo hard to share with your brother and I think you still worry that he will get more than you. It must be scary to think that I might give him more than you or maybe you even worry that I love him more than you.'

'When you saw the supply teacher you didn't feel safe, and you went to hide in the cloakroom and distracted yourself by looking through bags. Gosh, school is so scary for you sometimes. So difficult and scary.'

'I'm so sorry that Mum/Dad didn't come today. Oh, darling, you must be so confused. Maybe you're sad and angry too. It doesn't make sense why they didn't come and now you have all these feelings. This doesn't make sense and I want to be here for you.'

The temptation after giving our children empathy is to go too quickly into fixing or problem-solving but staying with the connection to feelings longer does a better job of conveying to the children that you can tolerate and handle their feelings and that those feelings do not mean that your child is bad, mad or worthless. As a therapist, I still have to work hard to stay with feelings sometimes, not because I'm worried or overwhelmed by the feelings myself, but because it's painful to see others in pain. Mostly, our drive to make it better for a child, just as we would if they cut their knee or broke their arm, is because we want to take their pain away. We'd be pretty dreadful parents if our child sustained a physical injury and all we did was empathize about how much it hurt, how much blood there was or how S-shaped their forearm was. Yes, we would empathize but we'd bloody well crack on and jump into action, getting tissues, swabbing, plastering, carrying, driving-to-hospitaling. We would *do* something for physical pain and when it comes to emotional pain, our default is to do something too. Remind them of what's going well. Tell them that they're not rubbish at maths. Give advice. Empathy isn't that stuff because it's just *being* with the feelings. There is a great deal of practical advice in this book and that is intentional but therapeutic parenting is also about slowing down, pressing pause, breathing it through, letting it rest.

A word on traditional parenting

Sticker/star charts, pegs moving between smiley sunshine and stormy clouds, time out, naughty steps, rewards and sanctions (such as grounding, removal of technology/TV, 'earning' money or toys, removal of money or toys, treats related to desirable behaviour) all make for popular, traditional parenting (in the past 20 years since we moved on from corporal punishment, seen-and-not-heard, and wait-til-your-Dad-gets-home stuff).

As a child of traditional parenting, I was a firm supporter in my adult years for some time. The whole, 'it never did me any harm' coupled with the huge love and respect I had for my mum and dad meant it took me a while to come around to an alternative idea, but the second our first foster child arrived, I quickly changed my view and even got to the point where I felt that my birth children would benefit from therapeutic parenting too. I still remember the day when one of my birth kids said, 'Mummy, I've got a maths test today. I'm so rubbish at maths.' I started to say, 'No, of course you can do this, you're great at maths' but found myself saying instead, 'Oh love, you feel rubbish at maths. No wonder you're worried about the test. I'm sorry you feel that way. That sucks. I know you'll try hard and that is good enough for me.'

I think the latter response was way more helpful than the former. But that's not to say that all aspects of traditional parenting are wrong or unhelpful with 'neurotypical', well-attached kids. It's just dreadful for traumatized kids. Why? I hope I can explain.

Shaming

Naughty steps, sad faces, dark clouds have *real* meaning for our children. It absolutely confirms their own sense of badness and worthlessness and prevents them from ever imagining a world where they could be any different. It's like convincing a dog that meat tastes nice. They already know and by giving them more meat you just keep the feeling alive. Yes, we need to let children know when they have done something unacceptable but the ways we can do that are covered by most of this book.

Excluding

Denying good times, nice things and positive experiences as a consequence for unwanted behaviour lets a child know they do not deserve them. Many, many times as a parent we rightly assess that our child does not deserve such things. But let me remind you of Father Christmas. It is culturally acceptable for us, as adults, to wield the scythe of Christmas ever-so-recent past over our children, telling them there will be nothing in their stocking unless they have been 'good' all year. *All year!* That is insane, given that few, if any, humans in history have managed a perfect behavioural year. Yet we waive our children's multiple misgivings and stack up the stockings regardless because...erm...it's Christmas. And it would be *awful* for our child to wake up to a stocking full of nothing. Or coal. For that festival in the year, we all yield and give our children lovely things regardless of their behaviour because of tradition and because of how utterly devastated our kids would be if we didn't. For that one day in the year, traditional, consequential parenting can do one because it's Christmas. What? Like, *what*??

For what it's worth, I am wholeheartedly a non-believer in teaching children that Father Christmas is a looming, judgemental git. To the point where, when my youngest child was in Year 4, I dropped her off at school but went into the hall with her little hand in mine to purchase the £1 Christmas Fayre ticket to see 'Father Christmas' a week later. A wonderful teaching assistant who knew my kids well and had worked at the school for years was selling the tickets. This lady, Mrs Burney, knew that my daughter was a hardworking child with impeccable manners and school-life contributions. However, as tradition dictates, when we approached her table of wholesome fundraising lies, she said to my daughter, 'Now, have you been a good girl or a baa...'

That's as far as we got. Because of the part of me that had helped other families limp through a tumultuous Christmas by telling children in sessions leading up to Christmas the following:

'You know. I think I need to tell you about the big lie about Father Christmas...' [Cue parents twitching of faces and massively increased heart rates.] What you need to know is that grown-ups like to tell kids that Father Christmas only comes to good children. Well, sweetheart, [hushed voice to increase affective intensity] the truth is that Father Christmas loves *all* children and always brings presents to *all* the children in the world. So, you need to understand that you and every child will get a gift from him this year.'

I wish I could convey the abject relief I see in children's faces and shoulders every time I tell them that. It's remarkable. So, going back to Mrs Burney asking my daughter about whether she'd been a good girl or a baa... I jumped in. Like a neurotic woman deprived of sleep for a week. 'CAN I STOP YOU THERE, MRS BURNEY!!?? [Mrs Burney stops, a little shocked at my gusto.] Because in our home, we *all* know that Father Christmas loves *aaaaaall* children and will bring stocking presents for everyone!'

Mrs Burney was lush, as always, and replied, 'Oh yes. So how many tickets would you like?'

But let's get back to my original point. Mostly, we as parents believe that 'bad behaviour' requires consequences. When you apply that schema to relatively regular, neurotypical kids, it usually doesn't do much or any damage. However, our children have lived lives where they have been emotionally and physically excluded, where anything they liked or loved got smashed up or taken away, or left at the previous foster home; they have lost loved ones, or been or felt displaced, or lived through a pandemic that took away everything they were expecting and has left them with anxiety. When we exclude them or take away something, they are just reminded of all that sadness. Instead, talking about what went wrong and repair avoids *reinforcing* feelings of being undeserving, bad and shameful.

Control battles

Because of *everything* that has already been said in this chapter, when it comes to fighting control battles with trauma, the trauma will always win. Yes, we must have boundaries and delineate between what is acceptable and what it is not but when we try to win control battles with consequences that hold up our children's poor self-worth, we generally lose. Taking away devices, grounding, withholding experiences and losing privileges are sadly no match for the power that trauma holds over these children. We can get into cycles of vying for control through means that are ineffective and make us feel more and more despondent rather than empowered. Sometimes taking the proverbial bull by the horns needs to be much more subtle than the metaphor suggests.

CHAPTER 11

Imperfectly Us

—— **Sally** ——

When Carly first starts working with a parent, she begins by explaining: 'In this work, I will be asking you to make changes, before we can expect your child to change.' I wouldn't relish having to deliver that message. Many come to the consulting room wanting a fix and our fighty, flippy, blamey brains don't want to contemplate that they may have to learn something new. Change makes us feel more vulnerable than we already do and takes energy that may be in short supply. Getting my head around the fact that the only power I have is to change how I approach a relationship has been very difficult but I must admit that it has helped many of my key relationships. A word of warning though – being prepared to learn and make changes is not the same as becoming a doormat or a punch bag. It has to be practised from a strong and assertive centre.

We've learned about the neuroscience and the biology of trauma and violence. We know a bit about states and capacity and responses to threat. We're starting to appreciate the stresses and triggers that result in dysregulated and violent behaviour. We've had some lightbulb moments and taken some strategies on board. We've taken steps to organize our lives and our interactions around our new knowledge. It all makes sense. And yet, no matter how much we learn and how hard we try, parenting our loved ones can be astonishingly difficult. We get it wrong, we blame ourselves and we wonder why we can't just pull ourselves together and do better.

There are two of us (at least) in this relationship. We foster carers, mothers, fathers, grandmothers, grandfathers, aunts, uncles, adoptive parents, single parents don't come to the relationship as blank slates.

We bring our life experiences, strengths, challenges, triggers, prejudices, values and ambitions to the party. Everyone does – and that includes teachers, social workers, therapists and politicians. There is no such thing as a neutral standpoint.

This chapter is all about why we matter, embracing the real us and parenting with what we've got.

We flight, fight, freeze too

I needed this pointing out to me and perhaps you will too. The threat detection system, capacity, states, triggers, all of that stuff – we have those things as well. We may have less flippy responses and more tools at our disposal to manage our responses, but nevertheless, we are working with our biology. It has kept us safe enough up until now.

Consider these questions:

1. How often are you operating outside your capacity?

2. How much of the time are you close to or in a state of flight, fight, freeze or flop?

3. How much stress is swishing around in your blood stream?

If you share your life with frequent violence, your answers to these questions will probably be a) often, b) often and c) loads. Is it any wonder that being a well-regulated, energetic, calm and unflustered model parent is sometimes or often out of reach?

What are our models of the world?

We all learn about how the world works from our very first experiences of living in it. I learned that those closest to me are basically trustworthy, that they won't hurt me, that I am safe, that my belongings are safe, that there is food available when I'm hungry and a dry towel to hand that doesn't smell of wet dog when I need one. Your first life lessons may have been similar or different.

I can no more unpick that learning than I can change my blood type – it is knitted into me. These are my models of how the world works – how relationships work, how people behave towards each other and my place in the world. Our brains use these models as shorthand to avoid having to think through every single situation from scratch.

When we find ourselves living with violence and aggression, our models of the world, which have served us so well, may no longer fit our new reality. Our brains struggle to compute the new normal. 'Hang on,' they say, 'the give and take way of doing things, which has worked for all previous close relationships is absolutely not working. What on this Earth is going on?'

When we kindly remind a child that it's time to have a shower or to please put the kitchen knife down and they respond by telling us to 'eff off', where do we go from there? Our brains don't know what to do with this unusual response. All that's left in their armoury is to sound the alarm and where do we go? Flight, fight or freeze. We run away, we shout back, we plead, or we freeze in horror.

Our model of the world assumes lots of other things too – that our purse or wallet is safe in our pocket, that we can take a child to a super-market without having to suffer abuse in the car, that scissors aren't weapons, that we can eat the last yoghurt in the fridge without fear of retribution, that we can sleep safely in our beds.

When our normal is so fundamentally and devastatingly challenged, it's a very big deal for our brains and bodies. Our safety is in question and as we know, safety and survival are the cards that trump everything. Not only that, our natural first response to extreme stress and danger is to escape from it – to flee. As caring and careful parents and carers, this is not usually a route open to us either. We can't abandon our child in the supermarket, or stop the car on a busy road and turf them out, or run from our frazzled lives (well, not too often). We live at the extreme *and* we are working hard to resist our biological urges. This is incredibly stressful for our poor, confused brains as they gaze out at their broken models of the world.

Let's give ourselves a bit of a break and decide where to go from here.

But first a thought about 'baggage'

The parts of ourselves that we bring to the relationship with our child are sometimes referred to as 'baggage'. 'You have your own baggage,' we are told. 'It's important to deal with your baggage.' I'm not keen on that term. It makes it seem inconsequential, silly, redundant, unimportant and something that can, by choice, be cast off. Our 'baggage' is not something separate from who we are, it is who we are. It's what makes us, us. It's our history, our upbringing, our experiences, the knocks we've had, our passions and interests and our values. Granted, some of it might not be that helpful in the circumstances we currently find ourselves in, but I think there's a case for embracing ourselves as a whole, accepting ourselves and working with what we've got. I'm not sure there's any other choice.

What I'm not saying is that we avoid the hard, personal work that comes with the territory of parenting distressed children. If we tend towards being hypercritical, for example, when we are under stress, we absolutely have to address why that is and where it comes from. If we are clinging on to certain values despite them being a poor fit for our family, we must ask ourselves where those values originate from and why they are so important to us. 'Is this my stuff, or is it theirs?' is a question we must come back to time and again.

It is tempting to believe that we can radically remould ourselves, in order to become the parent or carer our child needs us to be. It's true that there is a lot we can learn and many skills we can practise that will allow us to do a much better job. I've had to question a great many of my old beliefs about parenting, child development and family life and have become a much more empathic and conscious person as a result. It's not been easy. However, and it's a big however, we cannot fundamentally change the bones of who we are. I have often had to paddle hard against the strong current of my old, unreconstructed self. She is always lurking there somewhere, brandishing a highlighter pen and a college prospectus.

We are the best we've got. And that's why, although we can present a great set of principles and approaches about how to parent a child who behaves violently, there is no 'one size fits all' set of cast iron rules. There is an awful lot of personalization and self-acceptance involved.

Finding clarity in the mess

In the frazzled, confusing, noisy, frightening, messy lives that we share with our children, it can be very difficult to achieve any sense of clarity. When we are grappling with what is important, what to let go and how to keep everyone in our home safe, things can get rather muddy.

Every house has rules. In an averagely functioning home, a few rules may be explicit but most are just kind of understood and accepted and form the fabric of family life and the way it operates. Our homes might be quite different. The mess that is distress, violence and control stamps all over unwritten rules, so we are driven to make rules explicit. More undefined boundaries are crossed, so we define those boundaries. Before we know it, we are living in a web of rules and none of them stick.

One should not have to say out loud: 'Don't feed the dog cheese', 'Don't get up at 2am, switch all the lights on and have a shower', 'Don't use my bank card', but we do. It can feel as though setting out the rule will only increase the likelihood it will be broken. That's trauma, distress and control for you. But we can't live in homes with zero rules. It's not safe for a start, plus it's deeply unpleasant and stressful. It's also not real life.

Clarity is the key to unravelling the mess. It's the only way we are ever going to be able to decide on the absolute, rock-steady, non-negotiable rules in our home and carry them through. It's the only way we can carefully pick our battles. It's the only way we can captain this mutinous ship back to safe waters.

Most parents and carers never have to contemplate drawing up a non-negotiable list, so for starters, a fair amount of acceptance and recalibration is required that this is even a thing we have to do. That's before we even deal with the 'negotiables'.

It is not acceptable to hurt anyone in our home

For most parents and carers living with violence, this is usually the number one rule. You may need a few others as well, because of course, violent behaviour can come with some other pretty undesirable behaviours. We'll start here though.

Expressly stating this, with confidence and from a place of strength is for many a very difficult place to arrive at but it is this kind of clarity that can make all the difference. In order to reach the clarity, we may have to deal with an awful lot of complicated and difficult 'baggage' first. Achieving the necessary clarity is, in my experience, a lot about us.

Regaining our power

Living with violence and aggression can leave us feeling like powerless husks, at the mercy of the most horrendous behaviour. We can lose sight of ourselves and of hope for the future. Trying to regain order and peace in our homes is pretty impossible if we feel terrible about ourselves. In order to do and be our best, sometimes we have to remind ourselves of our talents and strengths, interests, knowledge and successes. We must flesh ourselves out again and reclaim our power.

This is not about reclaiming and exerting power in a controlling way, but standing strong as an adult, having the confidence to take charge and setting the tone in the house. Sounds easy, but how do we do it? Here are some ideas:

What are your strengths and achievements?
Take some time to reconnect with the best of yourself. What are you good at? What skills have you got? Drawing? Cooking? Chairing a meeting? Organizing an event? Taking care of people? Making things? Don't be shy. You may find yourself thinking: 'I used to be good at that' and surprise(!) you still are.

What do you enjoy doing?
This isn't to do with being good or talented, it's purely about enjoyment. Going to the cinema, knitting a pair of socks, putting up a shelf, making a model, brewing beer, growing carrots. Remember enjoying something? Enjoyment is what keeps us going through hard times.

What would your best friends and dearest family members say about you?
This is an exercise of the imagination and a reminder that you are not what your distressed loved one throws at you. Distress and trauma are not interested in the real you. Your friends and dear ones are. Listen to them and soak it up.

What is the Youness of You?
Those quirks that make you, you – your humour, the funny situations you've been in, the things that get under your skin that make no sense to anyone else – these are all your essentials. Embrace and love yourself, with confidence and pride.

The Fantasy Loser Parent

No matter how much they may pretend otherwise, distressed and traumatized children feel terrible about themselves. Living with a child who feels terrible about themselves can be strangely 'catching', so if you feel like a complete and utter loser, it may be worth considering where this is coming from. Our children may project their own sense of worthlessness on to us or they may conjure up a Fantasy Loser Parent and convince us that we are it. The FLP is a b***h, d**k, idiot, worthless, stupid, whatever. The FLP is not you, it's trauma's creation. Try not to be tricked into thinking you are the FLP.

The art of choosing our battles

Once we've achieved some clarity and strength and we've set out our absolute steadfast house rules, the next stage is to get good at choosing our battles. Oh how easy that sounds!

In violent homes, there will be a huge heap of 'issues' – the things that cause confrontation. Bedtimes, screen time, food, swearing, washing-up, pets, homework, wet towels, money. Like stones on a beach, there are a range of sizes from small pebbles to boulders. We have to decide which is the big, important stuff that we're going to stand strong on and which is the small stuff that we're going to let ride. This process is messy, personal, and an awful lot about (imperfect) us.

Why choosing our battles looks easy but isn't

Knowing that it is sensible to ignore swearing, loud music, night-time wanderings, domestic chaos or whatever it is, and deciding to rank them as small stuff, is a different matter to actually accepting and behaving as though they are small stuff. They are only small in comparison to the big stuff and the big stuff in our lives is really, really massive. In other people's homes, our small stuff would probably be the big stuff. In other words, some of what we are trying to accept isn't easy and we may falter and fail and that's part of how this works. I've had to do a fair amount of 'fake it til you make it' and it's helped. Even then, at the end of a hard day, I could still pick a fight over something I'd convinced myself I wasn't going to care about. This stuff can build up and burst out of us.

An example of something that I know is small stuff, but which builds and builds like a volcano inside me is towels. Already it sounds ridiculous. Who loses their shit over towels? Well, I do. You will no doubt have your own personal volcanoes. For now, let's paint a picture. Let's say there is an endless procession of soaking wet towels, from the bathroom to a bedroom floor, that remain there and moulder, until I retrieve them. If I were to have a reserve of energy and I'm loving life, I can retrieve the towels, smell test them, wash, dry and return them to the clean towel pile. When I'm tired and I've ignored 20 other small things, five big things and I'm pretending not to care about something I really, really do care about and I want a shower, and all the towels are soaked and smell of wet dog, I could start a riot. (I have, in the past, had to resort to drying myself with a tiny flannel, and even that looked as if it had been used for some purpose it was not designed for. This was after coming home from a trip to the police station. I coped with the trip to the police station really well. The flannel was the final straw.)

There is a lot about the so-called 'small stuff' that exposes our foibles and weak points and the lies we may tell ourselves. I'm cool, arty and liberal, right? I'm laid back, flexible and accommodating? It turns out, we may not be who we thought we were. Learning to parent can expose us to some uncomfortable truths about ourselves.

Why thinking about small stuff can turn us into radicals

Sorting the small stuff from the big stuff forces us to think very carefully about what really matters. Living in violent homes means that peace and harmony, mental wellbeing and relationships have to become our top priorities. This can put us at odds, not only with our imperfect selves, but with our extended family, community, culture and society.

Take for example, school and education. Everywhere we turn, the importance of doing homework, practising times tables together, reading and spelling and working hard and getting good grades is underlined. It's not uncommon in the later years of secondary education for children to be told 'these are the most important years of your life' and similar extreme and dire warnings about ending up on the scrap heap. Particularly for those parenting care-experienced children, the whole levelling up, making the most of life, educating your way out of the hand you were dealt is quite dominant and difficult to ignore.

But what if education is a source of great stress in our home? What if even mentioning homework results in extreme meltdowns and violence? Or what if the school day is so difficult that our child gets through the day by holding in their distress, right up until they walk in through the door, when it spills out?

We may have to radically rethink what being a good parent really is and relegate education, or some such other sacred cow, if not to the small stuff, at least to the medium stuff pile – something to focus on in the future if and when circumstances allow. Putting our child's mental health ahead of their formal education is, on the face of it, a no-brainer but that's not necessarily how it will be viewed from the outside. It can take great courage and fortitude to make the right decisions.

We may have to take radical decisions, when we are running short on courage and perseverance. This is yet another reason why parenting distressed children is more demanding than it seems. This extra paddling under the water line is barely noticeable, except to those doing the paddling.

Hello ego

When the pressures around school and education are coming from us, it's a different matter. If you value the opportunities that having a decent education opened up for you, or you would really like your child to achieve more than you did, or as well as you did, then there may be or definitely is some unpicking to do.

To what extent should we be reading across our life experiences to our child? Does it matter whether we did or didn't achieve at school? That really has very little relevance to the here-and-now. Our child is not us. They are not even an extension of us. It's tempting to try and experience some secondary glory through our children, but that's the work of the ego. The ego likes those shiny feelings, 'Look how great I am for raising such incredible children'.

If we're brave enough to spot the work of the ego and tell it to step out of the limelight, we can address what is needed in the here-and-now. What does our child need? Are we able to hold what we know about learning front and centre – that distressed anxious, scared children can't learn, or at least retain very little? If we can do that, and put safety and relationship first, we may well be on the right track. We will though have to drop or tone down some of our very deepest and strongest held beliefs and prejudices. Identifying where the pressure is coming from takes great honesty and bravery. And then we must see it for what it is, and sometimes it is all about us.

The ego can take charge in other areas of life as well – sports, activities, clubs, doing chores, learning to cook, good manners, eating certain foods, having a Saturday job – the things we may find ourselves and those around us quietly and politely boasting about. When our child's stress bucket is overflowing, pushing them to pursue these sorts of extra skills and activities can be what tips the balance. They can also become huge generators of conflict, especially when the reason we are trying to get our child to do these things is because we think they will be good for them (or us). Whenever our emotional attachment to some activity or behaviour or whatever is greater than our child's, that in my experience is where the landmines lie buried.

Catastrophizing

How often can we find ourselves joining some imaginary dots, for example between a child not eating vegetables, to them being sick and homeless? Or from refusing to take a shower to ending up in prison? Catastrophizing comes easily to many of us, especially when we live in high-drama homes. It takes place in education too. The 'This is the most important year of your life' pre-exam speech comes straight out of the catastrophe playbook. How much kinder (and truer) would it be to say: 'Look kids, it's way easier to get these exams now, but if you don't or can't there are other ways of carving out a successful life.'

There's a misconception I think that children are a bit dense and need things spelling out to them in stark and uncompromising terms – that they need to be hit over the head with a shovel. They appear not to be taking any notice of our polite naggings and so we raise the temperature until we are throwing around words like 'scrapheap' and 'prison'. No one needs to hear that.

Accepting the small stuff

Making the decision to relegate something to small stuff and actually carrying that through as though you really mean it are two very different skills. Some newly categorized small stuff may come easy. Other small stuff, no matter how hard you work at it, will continue to feel like big stuff. Where this is the case, I've found it best to acknowledge that I'm going to have to work extra hard and will often fail. Sometimes I will lose my shit over a wet towel and that's just the way it is. What I used to do was to hate on myself when this happened and get into a downward spiral of self-loathing.

'Look, I shouldn't have shouted about the towels but it really bugs me and you know that and sometimes I can't hold that in.'

This is the kind of verbal pressure-release I practised. On my A-game I would get in ahead of my meltdown.

'I'm pissed off about these towels. I'll go and be pissed off somewhere else.'

It's fair to say I have an uneasy truce with the towels and other hygiene- and filth-related situations.

Life hacks and emotional distance

Another way to reduce the pressure of absolute irritation is to think about hacks. Life hacks are ways of dealing with life's little annoyances by finding clever short-cuts. Life hacks are I think the way to go with a lot of this low-level, irritating crap. Here's that approach applied to the towels.

Since I realized that wet towels are small stuff in terms of living in a violent home, but nevertheless extremely irritating, I no longer saw myself as a petty idiot. I saw myself as a messy human, doing her best. I also acknowledged the time and energy it took to wash and moreover dry the towels – my time and energy, that I couldn't use for anything else. It's stolen time. Not sweating the small stuff can involve an awful lot of additional domestic tedium.

This is the life hack. I've reserved my own towel, which I don't keep in the bathroom. It is a different colour to the rest. I no longer care half as much about the other towels, because I have no need for them or emotional connection to them. I have no skin in the towel game. If there are five towels mouldering on the floor somewhere, I don't care nearly as much as I once did. Not caring is, I've learned, the way to go. It isn't not caring *for*, it's not caring *about*. I care deeply for my loved ones, but I don't care about the towels. This is not a completely foolproof system, because there are times when the livid scream monster breaks out of my mouth, but there we go.

This kind of life hack can be applied to many areas of conflict. Knowing your major sore points and finding creative ways to avoid them being jabbed at can reduce a lot of fighting.

There may be unexpected improvements to be gained from removing ourselves emotionally from a fight. Sometimes the fight has a purpose, and that purpose is to cause conflict. As we've set out, children who feel uncomfortable in a peaceful home environment may seek to create high drama, noise and fighting and having a parent or carer with a large number of exposed sore points really helps in achieving that. They know how to wind us up, not consciously, but they have a kind of emotional radar for this stuff. What really pisses us off is what gets targeted. With fewer opportunities to piss us off, there is less conflict and therefore less fighting and violence. Sometimes it isn't really about the towels.

TIP

Make a list of all the small stuff that really gets under your skin. It doesn't matter how stupid the small stuff seems.

Pick off the two most irritating.

Think of ways you could remove yourself from the battle, with zen-like grace. It may aid your regulation and make you more likely to pull out the good therapeutic moves when you really need to.

Grief

Living with violence as a parent involves a lot of sadness which can come at us from many different directions.

Grief comes in the gulf between what we imagined our lives would be like and the hard reality. There is another gulf too – that is the difference between the lives those around us are living and the one we live. It's not grief for the death of a real life or a person who has lived, but the death of hopes and dreams. It is an important and debilitating grief, that can feel all the more isolating because it isn't much talked about. Perhaps we are grieving some phantoms – the children we thought we would have, the marriage we thought would last, the friendships we'd imagined would prevail. Some of our relationships may not have survived. Other people may find our children too difficult to be around; they may have disagreed with us about the best way to parent our child. Conflict has a strange way of breeding conflict. And as our relationships buckle under the strain, we may become isolated and lonely. Grief and loneliness are extremely painful states.

The costs of sticking alongside a distressed child can be very great indeed. The lost opportunities for work, social life, hobbies and interests and holidays mount up. Our lives may become so dysfunctional and different from the lives of those around us that we can find it hard to function in the normal world. We may feel locked inside our own bubble of suffering, with nothing to talk about and little in the way of interest to show to others. The huge adjustments that our lives undergo change how we see the world. Some of these terrible losses improve with time and acceptance, but not all. Some stuff we may just have to live in an uneasy truce with. Some stuff we may have to put on the back burner for another time.

It won't always be like this

When it dawns on us that the only person who has the ability to change the landscape in our homes and set the tone is us, it can feel like a depressingly massive responsibility. And it doesn't feel fair. We may have to gather all of our strength to make this shift and it's hard. It's not only a steep and exhausting learning curve, it's about paddling against our history and our biology. It forces all the big questions – who are you? What do you want out of life? Can you make and stand by the difficult decisions?

All I can offer right now is this – the more practice you get, the easier it becomes. Children do learn new skills, take on strategies and eventually mature. There will come a time when you don't have to plan every decision and every response and when you don't have to parent like a master chess player. Life won't always be as tough as it is right now.

CHAPTER 12

Regulating Ourselves

—— Carly ——

As we have said multiple times so far, violence, aggression and distress in our children will send us briskly towards zones Amber and Red. Secondary trauma occurs when living with distressed aggression and violence and it's important to avoid this, but we've also been clear that being on the receiving end of this stuff is a trauma in itself – a primary trauma. Our own triggers, whatever they may be, are there for a reason. We encourage you to know and respect your triggers. In most families, folk never fully get to know all their triggers because their worlds are not tested to the brink of emotional or even physical extinction. Our triggers are about our models of the world and have kept us safe; they are not ridiculous. They might be ones that need reflection and challenge such as my 'enjoying food' trigger from Chapter 3 or they might be completely indispensable. Our bodies prepare for flight, fight and freeze as well as our children's. Animals in the wild don't get PTSD or bodily symptoms associated with trauma despite living as prey in stressful environments. Humans DO get these because once they experience trauma, they expect danger to occur at any time.

Most of us are not adapted to live like this. We are suited to short bursts of stress, not drowning in it but when we begin to drown in it, we fear it lurking around every corner. This chapter is about how *you* can stay regulated enough to manage what is happening in the moment, whichever zone that moment happens to be in.

Green Zone strategies

REMINDER! All the best strategies for regulating ourselves or our kids are exercises from the Green Zone.

Getting a break from trauma

Okay, so this is *so* obvious yet *so* underutilized. It is also vastly contingent on your friends and family network. Unless you have a shit-hot team of people around you and your child(ren), this will be extra tricky. Sometimes we fear the repercussions of our children being *anywhere* but home because it's just another place for them to hold in their angst, but we must try to take small, measured risks where we can.

Processing stress chemicals

Our responses to stress and threat are biological as well as emotional and the 'energy' generated in us because of triggers or responses to the stress/ threat needs discharging to maintain health. That might be exercise of any kind or regular massage or journalling or gardening or playing music or art. Whatever does the discharge for you, please do it.

Record events

It is not uncommon for us as adults to lose memories of violence or highly stressful experiences. It's because our brains are battling between the pain of being fully present during such an episode and a form of 'freeze' when we're completely disengaged from the experience. It can be helpful to document events and our associated feelings to 'mobilize' our experiences in positive ways, but also to spot triggers, patterns and so on. Chapters 3 and 20 are clear about the importance of the support network, and these people can also help you to deal with times of the week or year that you notice are triggering for your child. They can be available as a source of extra safety in your home or, as in our family, take your child out for a couple of hours every Wednesday night for a year because that child always seemed to get nettlesome that evening. Incidentally, we never figured out why (something to do with school, we think) but it didn't matter as our network helped us and all our children to remain safe by creating distance and distraction.

Couple relationships

It is a ubiquitous notion that having a 'united front' in parenting is a must. The difficulty with this is that it isn't easy with our individual values and the interplay of these with one another, let alone introducing the needs of a third human who happens to be our child. *Then* you might add a dollop of trauma into the mix and see how well we manage that united front. Not. Easy. And yet, still fundamental when trying to parent therapeutically. Not exposing disagreements in front of your child and caring for your partner relationship are imperative because otherwise, children feel less safe, more powerful and more responsible for what goes wrong. In my role as a dyadic developmental psychotherapist and as the female partner in therapeutic parenting, I was asked to write a brief statement for fellow fellas in the therapeutic parenting game. Here is what I wrote:

How therapeutic parenting can alienate blokes

When I start work with families I generally meet with both parents at the beginning of therapy. At this point, I burst any idea bubbles about me fixing their children or trying to 'make them better' and explain that not only are they (the parents) the main agent of change for their children's emotional development, but I will be aiming to help them adapt to their kid's emotional world. Of course, in time, I hope that our work together will help their child to feel better about themselves and less anxious in their relationships but the first thing I want to help change is the parents' approach to parenting. I want them to think about their own experiences of being parented and how that affects their responses to their kid(s). Having set that out, I have had one or two families that I've never seen again! For the majority who are brave enough to let me be part of their journey, the next bit of the trajectory looks a bit like this.

I do lots of work with the primary caregiver and the child or children because a) they're the ones spending most time with the kids and b) the other partner is at work earning money. In heterosexual relationships, that primary caregiver does tend to be the female partner.

Generally, the partner I am working with takes the lead in parenting style and increases their understanding of their child. They might also increase their connectedness to the child. They might start telling the other parent that they need to do parenting more like them and they might start saying things to the child that sound too soft, too woolly and disproportionate to the fact that they have just trashed the meal that took an hour to make. The other parent then might start to think and feel any number of the following:

- Therapy isn't working; why isn't my kid fixed yet?

- My kid prefers my partner.

- My kid is robbing me of my partner.

- I don't get what I'm 'supposed' to be doing.

- I'm useless/ineffectual as a parent and a partner.

- I can't do anything right so I'm not going to bother doing anything.

- This is all bullshit and I hate Carly.

- This is *not* what I hoped and dreamed for.

Guys, when you start to feel some of this stuff, can I ask, as a therapist and a mum, that you do the following. On the rare occasion that your children have *actually* gone to bed, pour yourself a drink and one for your partner. Sit down with them and tell them that they are doing an amazing job of trying to help your kids. Then explain that you don't really understand what they're doing and would like to know more. Read some books, go on some training (*everyone* who is reading this is already ticking that box, gold stars all round) and most importantly, come to a few therapy sessions – on your own, with your partner and with your kid.

Some of the worst outcomes I have seen for children occur when the parents have very different approaches to caring for the children and when the relationship between the parents is badly affected by their children's trauma.

Amber Zone strategies

This is all about remembering your safety plan and sticking with it. If you can stay on board in the Amber Zone while your child is in the Red Zone without joining them, that is a good thing and you're likely to be in the Amber Zone for biological safety reasons. If you can, try to maintain what we like to call a *mobilized presence*. This involves close-ish proximity while you stay on the move. Fold washing, deliver washing, wipe down kitchen sides, (pretend to) cook, play Xbox, talk at a calm but reasonably loud volume with your partner, play with the dog. If your child picks a fight or invites you to engage in Amber/Red Zone stuff, remember flight safety. Try to step out of the conflict rather than being drawn in. Body language is key, and you may have to fake it til you make it, exercising confident nonchalance even when you are quivering inside. Children can escalate if they sense we are scared or if we cry. Try not to cry in front of them out of desperation but also remember that if you do, you are human and we have all been there. This is *not* about 'showing weakness' per se as there is nothing weak about crying. It's that, in our experience, our children get even more triggered into shame when we cry, and this can result in further escalation through mockery or violence. If you can, slow the pace of an escalating exchange by 'umming' or saying, 'Ohoo, let me think about that while I'm making tea' or, 'Whoa, whoa, whoa, I'm happy to have this discussion but need some breathing space right now.'

Not being bounced or corralled into decisions is vital as we risk re-creating the same scenario over and over. A swift 'We're (by which you mean yourself if single or you and your partner if together) going to have to think about that before we reach an answer. We'll talk to you again about it tonight after we've had a chance to think.'

Red Zone

If you find yourself losing it and flipping your own lid, it's not where you want to be, but we all get there. The following responses should be deployed *rarely* and at times of critical urgency. Remember, we are biologically programmed to respond to threat and that means sometimes we go into the Red Zone. When we find ourselves here, beyond the realms of Amber flight safety, it's about trying to harness *safe energy* in the face of such challenging scenarios. It is possible to use our body and voice to counter our children's rage. Not cowing to it but using a non-aggressive affective counter. Reserving the noise for when we really need it. Harnessing the sense of losing your shit without doing it. Training your body to dysregulate safely rather than deny your biological responses. It involves using a mega affective tone of voice (one that conveys the emotion you want to convey) without any hurtful or shameful words. It might look like:

'Okay, I'm done! This is too much and you and I need to stop!'

'This is not okay and we need to settle our shit down!'

'Enough, enough, enough, let's leave it and talk tomorrow.'

'I'm done, you're done, we're leaving this until tomorrow.'

'I know I've lost it and I'm asking [neighbour/friend/auntie] to come over.'

'Stop now. This is not okay and we need to walk away.'

All these responses are about accessing *hyperarousal* in our capacity. In my not-so-finest hour, I remember screaming at Lisa, 'BUT WE LOVE YOU! WHY DON'T YOU GET IT?'

The idea/concept was right, but the words were too early. The sentiment was right and it shut the situation down, but I wasn't in control enough or rehearsed enough. Absolutely my bad. Though I really did love her and of course, I still do. If you do get through such an ordeal without losing it altogether, you can consider yourself to have achieved a massive mic-drop.

There are other occasions when going into *hypoarousal* is the better option. This is when, in the face of undeniable aggression and catastrophe, we get small. Not cowed, but having a deliberately, offline quiet presence. I'll give you an example. A young person was brought to therapy by their parent, who waited in the car for them while they had their session. The session lasted less than 20 minutes because he was so utterly wired and pumped about an up-coming situation that afternoon that he was terrified about (not that he would admit that). He left the session in an agitated state despite me keeping things as calm and unchallenging as possible. I do challenge children and parents in safe ways but not when they are in a mobilized psychological frenzy.

Given that he had got back into the car with his mum, I called his dad and found myself saying these words: 'Do not look him in the eye. Do not make conversation other than to reply to him as minimally as humanly possible.'

The dad understood completely and for those few hours it was the best action (or inaction) to take. Now, that could feel like a major cop-out, but it wasn't. This young person was so afraid and dysregulated that any attempt by his parents to dissuade him from his course of action would have led to violence. Hard core violence. Yes, it is not ideal and as was said earlier, we would only recommend operating in this way fleetingly and for a short time.

CHAPTER 13

Measures of Success

—— Sally ——

I t is important now and again to think about the measures of success to prevent us from chasing some unachievable nirvana. What are we aiming for? To live in complete peace and harmony, with a child who dutifully does homework, keeps their room tidy, eats healthily, helps out around the house and speaks respectfully to their adults in their lives at all times? It's unlikely, and unachievable.

Just what is achievable and how do we know when we've achieved it?

We will be aiming for something very different from what families around us would consider to be success. Indeed, some may look at our measures of success and consider them to be close to a proper failure. A big part of what allows us to carve out success for our child and us is ignoring what everyone else is doing. The rules and measures are very different in our homes from what they are in most other homes. It's a sod, but that's the way it is.

Success may be anything from 'my child no longer behaves violently' to 'the violence is just as bad as it ever was but I am coping with it better' and everything in between. Even feeling a little rush of optimism that we are trying out approaches and strategies that at last make sense is moving us a few steps forward on the road to success.

If you're feeling as though successes in your life might be very few and far between, don't forget that you are dealing with a phenomenon that few appreciate and even fewer could manage, let alone understand. You're already doing a massive thing here.

Possibly one of our most difficult challenges as parents and carers is accepting that to reduce the violence in our homes, we are going to have to drop the expectations in many other aspects of our lives. These are some of the trade-offs that you may have to contend with:

- Backing off from school-related matters in order that home is as peaceful a sanctuary as possible. This may mean never getting into the ring in terms of homework, revision or adherence to uniform rules. To others it may look as though you are a lax and disinterested parent, whereas what you are is a gold-standard one.

- Allowing loads more screen time than you otherwise would and that those around you consider to be acceptable.

- Accepting that bedrooms will be untidy, wet towels will lie on the floor and litter will not make it into the bin.

- Accepting that children may need to live outside the family home so that everyone is safe and relationships may be rebuilt.

Success and acceptance

Acceptance can be one of the hardest states to achieve and one that can fluctuate wildly, depending on how much we are soaking up at any one time. Even now, something that I thought I had long ago accepted can jump out from behind a tree and bite me on the arse. When our lives diverge from other people's lives, in significant ways, there will always be reminders of that divergence: in casual conversations, television programmes, social media posts. There may be a feeling of faint hurt, like a scar being rubbed and an accompanying feeling of guilt that we can't feel unalloyed joy for someone else's good fortune. It's another situation where we must be kind to ourselves. It's also where having a support group to reach out to can help.

Progress

It isn't always easy to spot progress, particularly if things have gone from say 'absolutely unbearable' to 'fairly horrific'. This is why we gently nudge you to consider keeping some kind of record. Reading back over a diary or a rough collection of notes or looking through your photographs will open your eyes to how far you have travelled. You will appreciate how much you've learned, how much better you've become at not walking into a conflict and how many more strategies you are using. There will be reminders of times you pulled an incredible piece of parenting out of the bag. Those parenting wins were not wiped out by the days, weeks and months that followed, no matter how awful or not they were. Every win matters. When we talk about adjusting our measures of success, this is what we mean.

In our real lives, progress may look something like this:

- My child managed to finish the school year without being excluded.

- We went out to a fast-food restaurant for half an hour and it was enjoyable.

- He stayed in his room all weekend but there was no shouting.

- She sought me out and told me about an incident online.

- I now step away from a confrontation and calm myself down, most of the time.

These are still successes, even though they may seem small ones. Success grows slowly and is built on the foundation of small wins.

What you may begin to notice is that even in among violent episodes, you are building a deep and connected relationship with your child. You may realize that due to the efforts you are making to talk about emotions, predict triggers out loud, model healthy responses to stress, and repair after a fracture, your child is developing an emotional awareness and language that exceeds that of other children their age. You may allow yourself to begin to wonder whether, as the violence subsides, a sensitive and attuned child might emerge from out of the red mist. This is a long game.

Gold-level parenting is finding the right opportunities to spell out some of the successes, out loud, around our child, so that they get to feel a sense of progress as well. Not all children will be able to take direct compliments and praise, but there are ways of reporting a change in the emotional weather, without it being a direct, personal assessment.

'Things have been calmer in our home.'

'I enjoyed spending this weekend with you.'

'We're communicating better.'

'I noticed you were kind to that person.'

These are all statements that it can be easy to forget to say, especially when we have lived around a hornet's nest for a long time. Sometimes it's good to take a chance and say something out loud.

CHAPTER 14

Mopping Up and Repair

—— Sally ——

*P*icture this scenario. There has been the most horrific incident: walls were punched, belongings lie strewn across the floor, bruises are forming, ears ring from screamed insults. A strange and unsettling silence sits over the house like a heavy blanket of fog. You feel a strange, jangly exhaustion that your body can't let you give in to, because it doesn't feel safe enough to. The question is – what to do next?

Incidents happen, because they can't all be avoided or de-escalated, no matter how skilled adults are, or how hard they've been trying. And it's not always possible to keep the world out, whether that's school, friendship issues, social media, or a big scary life change.

When parents and carers are mired in post-incident shock, it is extremely difficult, if not impossible, to flip into therapeutic parent mode. That's not to say that 'in extremis' (hospital settings, police stations etc.) you will have any other choice. If you are forced to push down the feelings, fasten on your super-hero cloak and march on, you must schedule in time to process what has happened and allow the big, horrible feelings in. If you don't, they will get you in the end.

Repair is where the magic happens

If there is one silver lining, it's that a violent incident provides the opportunity to repair. Repair is the opposite of what our child will be expecting and this is one of the main reasons why repair is where the magic happens. Repair is about demonstrating the enduring nature of your relationship, optimism for the future, problem-solving, resilience and forgiveness. It's not about letting things go and smoothing things over and neither is it about strong-arming and shows of force, although both these avenues may feel tempting at the time.

We're going to step through how the repair process might work. It won't always (or perhaps ever) work as neatly as this suggests but it's a good, solid process to keep in mind. It seems complicated, but you will soon get the idea and develop ways of making it fit the situation, your style and your capacity at any given time. The starting point has become something of a favourite of mine.

1. Do nothing

Doing nothing may not come easily, accustomed as we become to being men and women of action. But doing nothing is where we must start, as long as everyone in the home is safe enough. Safe enough may mean there is still some shouting, breaking things and crying, but it's on the downward bend. When things are cooling down and heading from the Red Zone into Amber, it's important not to do anything that risks bringing the temperature back up again, despite how wronged we may feel. For a time, we must retreat to our bedrooms, sheds, garages and bathrooms and let the shock settle, allow the fragments of memory to gather and begin to process what just happened.

You will probably not have the opportunity to fully recover and will have to leave it for another time. Don't forget to do this. If you have a free afternoon in a couple of days' time, don't fill it with chores and arse ache, do something that will aid your recovery. If you can avoid it, do not get into recovery debt.

2. Slow it down

For the worriers among us, who have the overwhelming urge to make everything better as soon as possible, I pass on some valuable advice that I was given a long time ago. Sitting in pain and really feeling disconnection as a result of something we have done is an essential part of learning about relationships. If every time this happens, another person rushes to our rescue, to protect us from those feelings, we don't get to experience and then process the results of our actions. We don't get the chance to do a better job next time. This doesn't mean that we leave a tiny child alone and scared, because that would be cruel, but using our judgement, we must allow disconnection to be felt. Older children may benefit from longer periods of disconnection, especially if their coping mechanism, after lashing out, is to quickly make out everything is fine:

'What the hell is your problem? It was hours ago that I called you a c**t.'

'I didn't do anything. You're such a weakling.'

When violence breaks out regularly and incidents merge into each other, with no time between to process or repair, then we must apply the brakes. Living life at the chaotic speed dictated by our child's distress strips us of control and agency. If an older child controls the emotional temperature in the home and ultimately the freedom of expression and movement of everyone living there, they experience themselves as uncontrollable and dangerous, and learn that operating in this way is how you get people to do what you want them to. That's before we get into the damage that living like this does to the rest of the family.

To begin to take control of the speed at which incidents play out, try using clear and brief statements that describe what you see and feel. These are delivered assertively and seriously and most definitely not in a sing-song voice. 'I'm not messing around here,' is the message.

'That was not acceptable. I am not talking to you about your plans for the weekend right now.'

'When you left the house this morning, you called me a c**t. Now you're being all sweet. What's going on?'

Communicating over text or messaging can be experienced as a less confrontational way of applying the brakes:

'We need to talk about what happened this morning.'

'It's not okay to speak to me like that.'

'You're going to want to come home and pretend like nothing happened.'

'I don't feel like making up with you yet.'

If your older child gets some comfort from the constant chaos and confrontation and has a need to be in control, they may experience you slowing things down as extremely uncomfortable. There may be a period when things get worse. If you can, you could call this out too:

'I can see you need to forget incidents and move on really quickly.'

'I don't move on as quickly as you.'

If you are parenting as a couple, it is important to be alert to the ways in which your child may seek to quickly smooth things over with one of you, leaving the other out in the cold. Being on the same page and working as a team are, as ever, important principles for couples:

'What you said to Mum was wrong. Now I see you trying to cosy up to me. I'm not ready to make this right.'

3. Reassure

After a mega-incident, our child will feel like hell. They will have said and done things they are so ashamed of, they won't be able to bear recalling them. They may not remember some of the things. (They will, however, remember every stinking thing you said or did in response.) They are likely to be expecting you will give up on them/hate them/lay into them and so we are going to deal with this first. This is likely to be the very last thing we feel like embarking on, but we must. Some parts of this type of parenting are deep, deep fake.

When all is quiet and the storm has passed, we are going to stand at the threshold of wherever they have hunkered down and say something like: 'We're going to deal with what happened later. I need you to know I love you. Right now, I need some time to recover.'

And then you walk out, even if and especially if you are met with a 'f**k off' in response. That will be the shame needling the fight response. Shame would rather kick off another storm than sit with itself. Your statement of intended repair and ongoing 'no matter what' love will be mulled over, so leave it to work its magic.

There are a few variables, of course. The first being, what if the child involved is very young and can't be left to cope with a huge amount of shame on their own? You could narrate and maintain a safe proximity.

'I'm going to sit outside your room. Call when you're ready.'

'I'll come back and check on you in ten minutes.'

The speed of repair will have to be guided by their real and psychological age and capacity at the time.

4. Ensure that everyone is safe

Another variable is brothers, sister, cousins and other children in the home. Quite a lot of advice tends to ignore the presence of other children. I'd guess that most violent households have more than one child living in them.

If you are the only adult in the house, with more than one child, you will have to cover all the bases. The sibling or other child is going to need a lot of reassurance and proximity, at a time when you may feel like curling up and never speaking to anyone ever again. There are times when we have to pull our best parenting out of the bag when we least feel like it, and this is one of them.

In that cold, white shock after a situation, other children in the home need to know that we actively seek them out, keep them safe and comfort them. It is easy to fall into the trap of directing all our attention towards the child who has behaved violently, thereby leaving the other child or children alone with their fear. Sometimes it's worth taking a step back, out of our own heads, and really thinking about how we are expecting them to respond to the situation and what this might be teaching them. 'What just happened is *not okay*', we need to state strongly and clearly. 'I've got this' is also helpful, even when we don't feel as though we have. As their parent and protector, it is important that we convey that we have the ability to keep them safe. 'If he doesn't stop, we're getting out of here and calling the police' is also a way of calling time on a situation and demonstrating that you are in control. We'll cover more on parenting siblings in Chapter 16.

5. Begin the rebuild

When a relationship suffers damage, as all relationships do, that damage must be repaired somehow, if it is to endure. Repair is difficult because it involves facing down hurt and regret and putting ourselves in a vulnerable position. It's not hard to see why a distressed child would find this incredibly difficult and even a red-hot trigger.

It will not surprise you to learn that the repair will have to be initiated and managed by us, even when we are the injured party. You may have a trusted family therapist who can assist in the repair process following a major incident. Even then, you are going to have to do a lot of the leg work yourself.

In repairing, we not only mend the fracture, allowing the relationship to get back on track, we also teach our child valuable life skills. I wasn't that great at relational repair before embarking on the intensive parenting by experience course that I found myself on. I was too easily wounded, could nurse hurt for days and found it difficult to summon up the bravery to speak honestly and clearly, but it has got a lot easier with practice.

This is a way of thinking about repair that has helped me and it's about bridges. In a functional, adult relationship, the two parties are like the opposite banks of a river and our relationship is the bridge between us. Friends and partners usually build bridges gradually as we get to know each other, learn about each other's foibles and establish trust. When we experience a falling out or a disagreement, the bridge sustains some damage and must be repaired. If it sustains lots of damage and repairs aren't carried out, it will fall down. A strong bridge can withstand a bit of jumping around on. A weak, wobbly one will collapse under less pressure. Our lives are littered with broken and worn-out bridges, but most of us have some really strong, enduring and beautiful connections.

Many parent-child relationships blossom from the outset and others take more work. When we share our lives with highly triggered, angry, distressed children, we are very much operating at the 'take more work' end of the scale. Our bridges are going to need a lot of regular maintenance.

When the relational bridge between us has been broken, we are going to have to make the first move by beginning the rebuild from our side of the bank because our child will not know how to. They may not even believe the bridge can be rebuilt, assuming that it is lost forever, such is their lack of trust in others. They may seem to give up, to our eyes, very easily. They may not trust our first efforts to reach out. This can be because their experience of relationships may be that they inevitably end, so there's no point even trying. They will gradually learn, by watching us, that it is worth trying.

Our first move will depend on the child and the situation, but for sure it will not involve very much talking. In the movies, adults and children talk it out by saying just the right things at the right time, hug and move on, but let's forget about all that crap. If the child is in deep shame, the first move may look like this:

- Sitting on the end of the bed for a few minutes.

- Bringing the child a drink: 'I've made you a drink.'

- Bringing the child a cube of cheese: 'I thought you might like some cheese.'

- Sitting next to the child on the floor: 'That was tough.'

- Standing some distance away from the child: 'I'll bring you some food up a bit later.'

Notice that we do not loom over our child, ask questions or deliver a lecture. In deep shame, a child will be thinking: 'I'm a piece of shit, so why are you caring about me?' Painful though this is to hear, it is the response we are aiming for. 'I wonder why I am caring for you. Could it be that I actually love you?' If we're lucky, we get to have this conversation in real life and not in our heads.

We are trying to confound our child. Confounding someone, really putting them on the back foot, shocking them (in a good way) causes the brain to do a 'WTF'. It can't follow its established way of thinking because it won't compute and so it is forced to recompute. We want to force a recompute, so that eventually the brain doesn't jump straight to 'I'm a piece of shit' and 'There's no point trying to fix this'.

If the child has a heap of attitude, evidenced by maybe smirking, smart comments, posturing, trying to exert dominance, then they are not in the repair or Green Zone, but in Amber and possibly close to Red. Any effort on your part to repair may become increasingly desperate and indicative of the weakness of your position. Exhibiting weakness can in itself be triggering for children, because they see us floundering and not able to keep them safe. It may be that we are in a prolonged fight for dominance, with a child who is both desperate for dominance and desperately scared they will achieve it. It is crucial, in my experience, that we retain a kind of benevolent dominance. By this, I don't mean the muscley, mean variety, I mean a trustworthy adult presence that demonstrates: 'I've got your best interests at heart', 'I am a safe adult', 'I know what to do' and 'I act with integrity'.

Generally speaking, the timing of repair is important – too quick and the repair is shoddy or fake (and the child concludes that was easy, but didn't learn much); too slow and the child is left sitting in unbearable amounts of pain for too long. And if we attempt repair before *we* are ready it can all go horribly wrong. Again, this is where this type of parenting is something of an art form.

The first move is repeated again and again until it is possible to move towards repair as a two-way process. You may have to demonstrate that you are not going to give up. This part can take hours and lots of patience and creativity.

Younger children will pretty much need us to build most (but not all) of the bridge from our side to theirs. The more practice they get, the more bridge they will be able to build from their side, to meet ours. Older children may need you to start the process before they can begin but when they can initiate the repair themselves, you know you're making great progress.

6. Make sense

To enact any kind of meaningful repair, both parties must attempt to make sense of what happened. This isn't easy, not least because the parties may have different takes on what the incident was about. We're not trying to enforce our take on the event, but we must also be on the look-out for some truth-twisting. Taking responsibility for our shitty behaviour is difficult for all of us and distressed children may try all sorts of ways of avoiding it.

All we can do is describe the event as we saw it. A top parenting way of doing this is to tell it as a story that connects before the event, the event itself and after the event. It's a past-present-future way of making meaning through storytelling.

'You were happy playing, then something happened and you jumped on your brother and hit him.'

Make it short and don't include every detail. This is a synopsis. In narrative form, the events were an interruption of or a blip in normal life. The child is a good person who made a mistake. Forgiveness is real. Hope is possible.

Once the synopsis is established, we move into a load of wondering what on earth set off the event: 'You were happy and I was enjoying being with you and then that happened.'

If you don't know what the kick-off event was, or you are dealing with a general increase in violence, then you'll have to play detective, throw out some suggestions and see where they land. What isn't likely to be successful is asking 'why?' 'Why did you do that?' 'Why did you react like that?' They won't know and even if they do, they're not going to tell you, because 'why' is usually the opener to a lecture. We need to come at this carefully. It's about finessing the information out.

'You came home from school and I could see something wasn't right' could evolve into, 'Was it a difficult day?'

You may hear: 'I'm fine/it was fine'. Fine is a word I've learned to be wary of. It's a shutdown response and usually signifies things were far from fine.

If your child begins to give you clues to what set the event off, then we have to demonstrate we can take it, whatever the information is. You may hear something like:

'I got a detention at school.'

'My teacher is leaving.'

'My sister swore at me when you weren't looking.'

'Something's happened on social media.'

'It's unfair that you won't let me go to the park on my own.'

Whatever it is, we must respond with something like: 'Thanks for telling me.'

It is tempting at this point, when you have a sniff of information, to go hard at it to get at more. But this is when we should go slow. Pause. Let that information settle. What do you make of it? Where could you go with it? Sometimes leaving a pause after a 'thank you' gives our child time and encouragement to share a bit more.

As the conversation develops, we're looking at exploring and unpicking what happened, without judgement. This is not the same as making out that what happened was absolutely acceptable. We're trying to arrive at: 'I understand why that got to you. What you did was not acceptable' and then, 'Let's work out how to help you manage better next time.' For example: 'I understand you want to go to the park on your own. What you did when I said "no" was not right.' Some time later this could be followed with: 'What would you like about going there without me?' We explore the desire, we don't stamp on it ('you're way too young to go on your own, you can't be trusted' etc.). It may be that we have to think about allowing them to go on their own, for a short burst, or whatever. Or it might be completely out of the question. 'I'm going to have a think about how and when it might be possible for you to go for a bit on your own. It's still not acceptable to behave like you did' is an approach we may need to try.

The conversation may need to move in a different direction if, for example, you think it may be worth exploring your child's response to 'no': 'It's hard for you to hear "no".'

You could try leaving a long pause to see what emerges, 'I'm going to think about when I can say "yes" to you.'

You may then engineer situations where you say 'yes' in extravagant ways: 'Can I have a biscuit?' or, 'Oooh, just let me think about that. Hang on. Yes, you can. Hey, look at me saying "yes".'

This kind of humour doesn't work when either party is still in deep hurt, but with careful timing it can demonstrate that you are recovered and love them enough to be able to move to humour.

7. Make amends

As we learned in Chapter 10, Why Therapeutic Parenting?, we don't think in terms of punishment, but that doesn't mean there isn't sometimes a related consequence for whatever happened. A consequence could be:

- helping you to clear up the mess

- doing something thoughtful for the wronged party

- helping you with some kind of household job.

These are designed to allow for time spent together, doing something active and busy, with opportunities to talk more, have a tea break and admire the work once it's done. There may be situations when the event itself was the consequence and all you need to do is sit alongside your child in their shame, without judgement. Examples might be an incident that played out at school, or something resulting in a broken friendship.

If you are parenting as a couple, you can play a double-hander. Usually, one of you has taken the strain of an event and the other was away from the home, or not directly involved. If you were less involved, then you can carry out the repair and restitution process while your partner recovers. It could go something like this: 'Dad is sad because of what you did. He's going to need some time on his own. Later we will make him a nice drink as a way of saying "sorry".'

This isn't carried out as though you are kind of 'rescuing' your partner as it may weaken them in the eyes of your child. Another potential pitfall to avoid is 'ganging up' against your partner ('Yeah, Dad was out of order, he should have let you do that'). When we're parenting amid violent behaviour, we can fall into dangerous patterns if we're not working together as adults. Some children have learned that manipulating adults gets them what they need and they can be very accomplished and convincing. It's not nice to say that, but it's true.

8. Deal with unfinished business

Once an incident has been dealt with, we would usually like to move on and forget about it. Painful memories fade for a good reason – we can't live in the cumulative pain of the past. However, it isn't always a great idea to deal with a situation and then never talk of it again. It creates a further shame, because it seems too hot to handle. The day after an event and then a few days after that, it's worth revisiting the event in a non-confrontational way.

'I know that was a hard day. How are you doing?'

'Have you had any thoughts about what happened?'

'We're going to clear up the garden together this weekend, remember?'

I haven't always been very good at doing this, but I have tried.

Gold-level parenting is seeing a similar situation on the horizon to the one that set off the violent incident and calling it out:

'You've been invited to a party? Let's work out how we can make it a success this time.'

'You've got a day off school next week so I've taken a day's leave and we're going to do something together.'

'It's your sister's birthday soon. I know it'll be difficult for you so here's what's going to happen.'

It's hard work and involves a lot of mental chess playing, but keeping our child in mind, anticipating their difficulties and putting strategies for success in place is an exceptionally successful way of avoiding violence and of building life skills.

9. Replace or not replace?

When belongings get broken, there is an added consideration in the repair process – literally and metaphorically. Our decisions depend on what was broken, its value and who it belongs to. Here are some of the variations and how we might approach them.

BELONGINGS

When something that belongs to a member of the household has got broken, say a favourite cup or a toy, I think it's fair to get a replacement and for the protagonist to either pay for it, or do something helpful around the house to pay for it. 'You can't go around breaking people's treasures without consequence' is the lesson we are trying to instil, plus 'It is possible to make amends'. If the breakage was an accident, then perhaps we replace the item and deliver an 'it's okay, accidents happen' message.

DAMAGE TO THE HOUSE

Let's say a door frame, window pane or wall is damaged. It's not cata-strophic, but it's inconvenient and acts as a constant reminder of the incident. In some of our households we have to get used to living with an amount of damage, because either we can't keep up with the repairs, we don't have the spare cash to pay for them or we are exhausted. If possible, it's best to repair things, so they are not generating more and more shame. You will have to decide if the wrecker of things puts some money towards the repair, or helps with it. What doesn't usually work out is lumbering our child with a substantial debt that they can't ever hope to pay off. They will probably feel despondent, which will only fuel more bad feelings. Having said all this, we once left a broken window in place for two years, because we just didn't have the capacity to fix it.

TECH

The items with the most real and emotional value in our homes are often mobile phones, tablets and games consoles. In many families, the breakage of a mobile phone will unleash all sorts of misery that will rain down on everyone for days and weeks. There may be demands made that you replace the phone immediately, attempts to access someone else's phone or even a secretive contract or purchase. It can present like an addiction. Cleverer folk than me will decide whether it is a real addiction or not, but all I'll say is, if there was a new iPhone lying beside my dying body, I wouldn't fancy my chances.

Let's say your child threw their phone in utter frustration, called you something vile, kicked a sibling and pulled a door off its hinges, all because something took place on social media that you will never get to the bottom of. Excruciating though it may be, it's probably time for a social media break. You'll have to judge how quickly you replace or fix the phone, but I'd say some waiting time is important and is a consequence in itself. It can also slow down a cycle of crisis, if you are in one. Move fast and break things? Hang on a minute.

If this is your life, I advise that you become acquainted with the sellers of second-hand tech. There are plenty offering reconditioned phones with warranties at a fraction of the gazillions that a new one costs. If a second-hand phone gets broken, you may feel way less emotionally bruised than if a brand-new, expensive one does. Generally, I've tried to remove as much emotional baggage from belongings as I can. If I don't care about them, I can usually manage my response. If I've shelled out hundreds of pounds for something and it gets hurled at a wall, it's going to really get to me.

10. Reaffirm the boundaries

Once the storm has passed, we've cleared up the immediate mess and our dear ones are regulated (or as regulated as they can be), it's time to reaffirm the boundaries. I think of it as hammering the fence posts back in. Sometimes they need to be moved a bit, one way or the other, because we're learning as we go along.

We may need to have the Boundary Conversation, again. Hold this at a time and place that is most likely to result in success, whether that's on a car journey, in a café, or wherever works for you. Practise what you are going to say, and keep it brief and assertive.

'I need you to know this. I will not allow anyone in our home to be hurt. If you hurt me or your mum or your sister again there will be consequences.'

'I need you to know this. If you hurt or threaten anyone in our home again, I will call the police.'

'If you break your phone again, I will not be paying for it to be repaired.'

This conversation only makes sense if we are at the same time supporting our child – listening to and empathizing with their difficulties, teaching them different responses, reducing the stress in their lives that we are able to, and all the other good work. Without this, you can bang in those boundary posts as energetically as you like, but they will fall over.

Repairing our smashed-up relationship and our smashed-up home, over and over again, is relentless and exceptionally hard work. It brings with it a special kind of pain and exhaustion. But life won't always be like it is now. It's hard to imagine, but it's true. Our loved ones will venture into the world, carrying what we have taught them. That learning may take some time to show itself, but it is there. One day you will have the time and energy to fix everything – your home, your other relationships and yourself, and the fixes will hold. Your poor battered home will recover and so will you.

Summary

- Do nothing.

- Slow it down.

- Reassure.

- Ensure that everyone is safe.

- Begin the rebuild.

- Make sense.

- Make amends.

- Deal with unfinished business.

- Replace or not replace?

- Reaffirm the boundaries.

CHAPTER 15

Involving Children in Problem-Solving

—— Carly ——

Like many bewildered-yet-logical parents of children who express distress through violence, I (by this I mean, Mr K) purchased and hung a punch bag in our garage. 'There!' We triumphantly exclaimed to Lisa, 'Now when you feel angry, you can punch seven bails out of that!' Our intentions were good and we'd talked to her about giving it a go. She agreed, but of course, it never worked.

Children in the Amber and Red Zone rarely have the reflective capacity to consider how hitting an object designed to be hit is better than the person or wall or door next to them. Neither do inanimate garage-housed punch bags activate their attachment system and all the complications that go with this. For these very reasons, problem-solving with your child might not always be successful. Children and young people are often well intentioned in their own responses to violence. 'I'm sorry', 'I won't do it again', 'I don't want to hurt you', 'I didn't mean it'. As I've said before, I don't believe that children who respond to distress, anxiety and fear are intentionally violent. This chapter is about ways we can get children as on board as possible to manage and control their own responses. The earlier we begin with this age-wise, the better. Like I said in the introduction, my hope is that some families will read this early enough to begin tackling aggression and violence as soon as it begins to surface.

Developing an emotionally age-specific shared language with our children to describe what happens to us when we get sad, angry, anxious and excited is a good place to start if we want to partner with our children in tackling aggression. It's especially helpful if we can locate feelings within children's bodies. Here are some ways we can talk to children about that. Key to this is normalizing their feelings where that applies. For example:

> 'It makes sense that you get sad/angry when children call you a "heavy b***ard/adopted weirdo/pizza face/rich Tory/retard", because *it is not* okay to be called that. It gives you a sinking feeling in your stomach.'

> 'Of course, you are sad. Someone you loved died and now the sad is so big it makes you want to not get out of bed.'

> 'Yes, you are worried about school camp because of who you might have to share a dorm with. It's hurting your head.'

> 'I get it. You wanted to really hurt him because he said your birth mum didn't want you. You wanted to hurt him with your fists like he hurt you with his words.'

For younger children
Fizzy high/Fizzy low/Just right
This is essentially a way to talk about capacity using younger language. Helping children locate where these are/how they feel in their body can increase their own awareness.

Super brain/Sponge brain/Dinosaur brain[9]
This model helps children understand how their brains sense something as *safe* or *unsafe* based on all their previous experience.

Back-to-front learning
This is for children who have experienced significant early years trauma (abuse and/or neglect). The phrase came from one child I worked with many years ago. In the session with her parents when we talked about how her new parents were doing things differently from any of her birth or foster parents and how this was taking some getting used to – perhaps how hard this was for her – she suddenly said, 'Yeah, I've got back-to-front parents because I am an upside-down kid!'

What this child said in that moment was remarkably insightful and sent me on a trend of employing this theme in future work with families. We can explain to them how they, as babies and small children, had to learn to survive and therefore had to learn 'grown-up' ways of being rather than child-like ways of being. For those who have lived this way, we can talk about how, in the here-and-now, their new/safe families are trying to help them to learn how to be a child. For instance, learning how to make friends, interact with peers, relinquish constant control, ask for what they want/need rather than stating they will get this for themselves.

Other areas that 'back-to-front' children need help with include relinquishing parental roles over younger siblings, disentangling their own identity from siblings, asking for help, anything toilet related, age-related self-care (who gives a crap about brushing teeth when you're growing up in survival mode), complete disconnection from physical or emotional pain, maintaining invisibility and, of course, violence as a means of preserving self-safety.

Are you asking me or telling me?

This is more like a sub-section of back-to-front learning. I want you to imagine me doing an initial parent and child therapy session. There aren't tons of toys or other stimulants, but I have a few things around the room such as fiddle toys and soft balls. Some children tentatively allude to stuff they want to explore or sit rigid and stare at what they would like to do. I say something like, 'It looks as if you might want to explore my box of fiddle toys' or, 'It seems that you might want to ask to play with something.'

At the other end of the spectrum, I have children who stride into the room, pick up everything and say, 'I'm going to play with this ball!' or they say to their parent, 'Rub my back!'

In either case, I get a dialogue going about how hard it is for them to ask for what they want or need. 'Ohoo,' I say, 'it feels as if you're letting us know that you want to play with the ball. Can you find the words for that? We can help, if you like?'

That's quite a behavioural approach but does serve to awaken them to their own process. The 'deeper' work looks like this:

'Wow, I see you really want to play a game but it's so hard for you to ask Mummy/Daddy about whether that's okay. Whoa, that makes sense because you're not used to being able to let adults know that you need something. You've always had to rely on yourself and now you have these parents who want to help you. Gosh, that must be hard to do! So hard.'

At the family home, the classic example is:

Child: 'I'm getting a snack from the fridge.'

Parent: 'Hmmmm, are you asking me or telling me?'

Child: [bemused look] 'Um, asking you?'

Parent: 'Great, can you turn that into a question? You do that by saying, "Can I have a snack?"'

The emphasis here is on the child being able to ask the question. We can get a bit hung up on there being pleases and thank yous but frankly, I'm not bothered about that. The more important issue is helping the child to trust us enough to *ask us* for what they want or need. A child may battle for years over this but empathizing with this battle is key to helping them learn to trust adults who are trying to parent them and keep them safe.

Recognizing signs

As we 'learn' our children, we recognize their triggers before they do, and part of our role is increasing their awareness of these triggers, letting them know what they find difficult and 'scaffolding' it. The reason for returning to this is that, if we can get into a 'flow' of dialogue about what our children find difficult, we stand a chance of being able to predict when this will happen and how our children might manage the situation. *Any* difficult scenario can be better responded to if we have thought ahead about it in the Green Zone. I'll give you an example. Whenever we had a school holiday or went away anywhere, I began to notice that when we came home, interested and caring folk would ask Lisa, 'How was your holiday?' or, 'What did you get up to in half term?'

At this point, Lisa would absolutely freeze and have no idea what to say. As time went on, she would shoot me a look as if to say: 'Heeelp! I don't know what to say!'

After approximately two years of her being with us, I realized that Lisa panicked in those situations and didn't know how to respond or what to say because of her ability to recall and to verbalize to others. So, I tried something. At the end of a holiday, I said to Lisa:

'Hey, I reckon that when we get back home lots of people will ask you about our holiday. I've noticed that when that happens it's hard for you to remember and say what we did. So how about we think about your favourite part of the holiday now so that will be easier for you when people ask.'

We did that and even rehearsed it. I can still remember the moment a few days later when someone asked her how her holiday was and she said, 'It was good. My favourite bit was the swimming pool and the food!'

Bloody brilliant. No anxiety or frozenness. No shame to spark aggression.

I have a gap or two

Ross Greene[10] (2021), a child psychologist and author, talks about children who lack the skills to behave or do well. They're challenging because they can't do these things. Can't, not won't. When the demands put on them outstrip the skills they have to do a task, children can feel shame and, as we've said, shame is the rocket fuel for aggression and violence. Some of the children we work and live with genuinely lack problem-solving, decision-making, cause-and-effect thinking and procedural functioning skills. If we identify where our children have such gaps, we can start a dialogue with them around these gaps. The example I gave in the previous paragraph showed me identifying a gap in Lisa's recall and language skills and giving her the skills to manage the demands put on her when asked about her holiday. Thinking through basic tasks such as asking a child to take the recycling outside and sort it goes like this: 'What skills do we need to do the recycling? Are you going to manage it all in one go or will you need to take two trips? Is it light outside or will you need a torch to see? Are you afraid of the dark?'

Being angry with the right person

We've talked a lot about how distressed-based violence is often expressed towards us as parents because of emotional pressure that has nothing to do with us. It's important that we try to disentangle some of this anger from us by helping our child be mad or upset with who they're actually upset with. Sometimes we do this reflectively in the Green Zone, talking with children about who they are angry with (possibly during a repair) and how they can safely express this or how we can help with this. You might need to find the words for them, such as, 'I bet you wish you could tell Ruby what a mean horrible girl she is and how much she hurts your feelings' or, 'I know you can't show your dad/mum how angry you are with them. I think I get a lot of the anger that belongs to them and I think we need to find ways of sending some their way.'

Of course, it's not always possible for children to be angry with people who are not a part of their life, or they may have huge anxiety about being able to tell people that they're angry, so writing letters that they'll never send or drawing pictures of how angry they are can help. When we detect that anger being thrown at us in the Amber Zone doesn't belong to us, a quick, clear statement of that fact is helpful. It might not even make a difference to the level of anger or de-escalate it, but it does help the child be more aware of what's happening and to draw a boundary between you and the cause of their distress. Something along the lines of:

'Okay, you're really angry right now. I don't think it's about me but I'm here to help.'

'I'm backing off. You're angry about something that isn't to do with me.'

'I've said something to set you off but it feels as if something else is going on.'

'I want to help you. I don't think this is really about your hair.'

The four Fs

For once, this isn't about swearing! When our children are younger, we make tons of guesses about what's going on for them. Some of us even become wizards at reading every verbal and non-verbal cue our child is emitting. That's all great stuff but we run the risk of our children getting fed up with us always being right and even making them feel inadequate. This is a reflection technique that can be used with children in the Green Zone and seeks to bring the child on board in terms of how they read a situation. It takes a bit of time and, like everything in this book, it's another tool you can use, or not. It works better with children who have good reflective skills and are not constantly on the verge of shame.

It's definitely got its place as a good reflection tool both for parents/ professionals and children/young people alike. The Four Fs are:

- Facts
- Feelings
- Findings
- Future.

When something has gone wrong, particularly where it's a cyclic issue, we can use this to first make a note of all the facts. Sounds easy but trying to keep emotion or opinion out of it is harder than you think. Then we look at how everyone felt in relation to the facts. Next, it's the sense we can make about the facts and feeling and what we learn from these. The future is about what we can put in place or do differently for a better outcome next time. Here is an example:

Facts – Mother: Our family went for a walk with another family. During the walk, Jacob (child of the other family) and you (daughter) talked about playing football together previously, a game that was a draw. Jacob kept saying that he had really won that game. He gave different reasons for why he thought this was true. I noticed this happened and reminded Jacob a couple of times that I was with you both when you played that game and that it had certainly been fair. Later in the day you and Jacob played football again and I was referee. You won the game. I suggested that we also do a penalty shootout, which Jacob won.

Daughter: I heard you tell Jacob that we drew and the game was fair, but you didn't notice all the times he said it. He wouldn't stop saying that he'd won.

Mother: Later in the evening when it was just our family watching a film, you said you didn't like the film and didn't want to watch it. You could not settle, and we said you seemed angry. You said you wanted to play football and we said that you couldn't as it was very late and dark outside and wondered if there was something else bothering you. You became aggressive and there was a lot of shouting and trying to hurt yourself and me, which I tried to stop. I did some shouting too after a while. We talked about what was bothering you and after some time

I guessed that it was to do with what Jacob had said and how he had behaved. You cried and I hugged you.

Feelings – Daughter: I was upset and angry about what Jacob was saying but I didn't tell you at the time. I felt like I was supposed to be friendly to Jacob and kind of as if he was allowed to say that stuff to me. I really love football and often boys exclude me or are unkind to me when I try to play with them, which hurts my feelings, and it felt the same with how Jacob was talking to me.

Mother: I was really proud of you for trying to be kind to Jacob. I was a bit annoyed at him for what he said about your last game. I feel Jacob really struggles with losing so I suggested the penalty shootout, but I wanted to be fair so stuck up for you on the walk and celebrated when you won the game afterwards. I feel bad that I didn't hear everything he said to you on the walk. I wish you had felt able to tell me that he was keeping on about it. I would have liked to help more, just as I always do.

Findings – Daughter: I didn't like what Jacob was saying, but I wanted to try to be kind to him and let his mum talk to you. I didn't ask for help from you for that reason. Then the sad and angry feelings kept bubbling and in the evening, I couldn't settle with the film. All I could say was that I wanted to play football and you saying no meant that I got aggressive. I don't really want to hurt you.

Mother: He was upsetting you with his comments and although I noticed some of this and challenged him, he kept on, but I didn't hear it. You often have boys be mean to you about football and it felt this way on the walk. When we played again after the walk and you beat him, maybe it felt as if you'd shown him your skill but then I suggested the shootout, which he won and that took some of the good feelings you had about your win away. I really didn't want you to feel that way and I really wish I'd known at the time about the unfair comments he was making because I would have done something about it.

Future – Mother: It's so important that you ask me for help, no matter where we are or what we are doing. Those feelings of being pushed round by boys in football are huge and we need to find a way to get you to ask for help. Do you have any ideas? I think I'll stay much closer to you if I think that might be happening but there might be other times when you need my help too if we're out and about. It seems as if you need to let me know you need help as soon as you get the feeling.

Daughter: I'm not sure but maybe you staying nearer will help. Maybe if I say I need the toilet you can come with me and then I'll be able to tell you what's up.

This approach comes from the world of social pedagogy, which seeks to provide a holistic, relationship-based way of working in care and educational settings. This particular technique can work especially well if a third adult, one unconnected with the incident itself, can mediate and help keep each 'section' of the work clean.

PART 4

Influences and Specific Challenges

CHAPTER 16

Brothers and Sisters

—— **Sally** ——

Whether you are part of a regular, blended, step, foster or adoptive family, there is a fair chance that you will be parenting other children alongside the child who is struggling with distressed and violent behaviour. There's also a fair chance that the dynamics in your home – the relationships your children have with each other as well as you – will be complicated. Violence and the reasons for it affect everyone in the home and yet it is difficult to hold the needs of all family members in mind. Violence has a habit of taking up all the oxygen. Many parents and carers will be troubled by a perpetual worry that their other children are not being served well and may even be damaged by witnessing and perhaps even experiencing violence in their home.

We offer some ways of thinking about violence in the context of the family, with the knowledge that these are impossible situations to get entirely right. For ease, I've used the terms Child A to mean the child struggling with distressed behaviour and Child B to collectively mean the other children living in your home, either full or part time. It is, of course, rarely this straightforward.

Redirect your attention

Undesirable though it is, violent behaviour is a pretty effective way of holding an adult's beam of attention. This makes it kind of rewarding – in an 'it's better to have some attention, rather than none' kind of way. The problem is, while the child is getting their need satisfied and we're running around in circles, what and who are we ignoring and what patterns are we reinforcing?

Child A, whose distressed violence dominates the home, not only soaks up the attention of the adults, but their poor self-view is reinforced too. I know I'm rubbish, I've behaved in a rubbish way and the negative attention this has attracted is telling me I am rubbish. The family may be locked into this self-perpetuating cycle.

If Child B is scared by the distressed violence, which is sometimes aimed in their direction, instead of competing, they may cope and survive by being quiet and getting on with things. They may have learned to expect that when Child A kicks off, the adults will run in Child A's direction, leaving them alone, for as long as it takes. They learn that their fear and other needs are secondary and don't matter. They may learn that their chances of not being hurt increase if they hide under the radar and keep themselves to themselves. They may also learn different strategies to gain attention or to ease the unbearable tension in the home, such as being entertaining or compliant. The problem for adults is that these strategies work for us – what a relief to have one child who is able to smile and laugh and bring us a biscuit when we need one, or whose needs barely figure in our minds when we are knee-deep in crisis. The problem for all the Child Bs out there is that they are learning patterns of behaviour and about their worth and place in society that they may take forward into their adult lives.

'My needs are secondary.'

'If I want the attention of others, I must only display the best of myself.'

'I must try not to be noticed if I want to be safe.'

In subtle ways, the space-taking, traumatic ways of Child A traumatize Child B. We can avoid the problematic terminology as much as we like, but the reality is that Child B is living with domestic violence, which is toxically stressful. Neither Child A nor Child B are choosing to operate in these ways. It's not a matter of being sneaky or manipulative, which are words that adults sometimes use to interpret and evaluate what are just survival mechanisms. All children would use these mechanisms, should they have the misfortune to need to do so.

Many of us have fallen into the trap set by trauma and beaten ourselves up because we think we've ruined our child's lives by not understanding or seeing what was going on. If that's what you're doing now, then remember that you are at the mercy of some extremely powerful and wily survival drives. We begin to counter these and better meet the needs of all our children by first gaining knowledge. That's what you are doing right now. When we understand, we can change our behaviour and create a healthier dynamic in our homes.

CHEESY TIP

If you are experiencing terrible feelings of regret for not knowing about all this years ago, remember this –

the best time to start doing something differently is now.

Forgive yourself and move on.

When violence is present in a multi-child household, the ask on parents is massive. Here are some suggestions for making small but important changes and not heaping on the self-guilt.

Force your attention to your quiet Child B

To do this, you may have to train yourself. As a situation begins to rumble ask yourself: 'How is my quiet child doing?' and search them out. Useful openers are: 'Just checking in on you. How are you doing? How was your day?' and, 'It looks like things are going to get tricky. I'm here.'

Have Green Zone conversations with Child B

Talk to Child B during quiet times about how they feel when an incident takes place and what you are going to do to support them: 'I realize I've been ignoring you when the violence starts. I'm going to try really hard not to do that any more.'

Narrate your intentions

If an incident erupts and Child B gets hurt, narrate your intention to both children: 'I'm taking care of you, Child B. That was not right. Child A, you don't have my attention right now.'

Listen to Child B

Child B may have a knack of hitting the nail on the head. 'They always ruin my birthday.' 'They get away with stuff I wouldn't get away with.' 'You don't like spending time with me.' 'You only ever think about my brother.' We may be forced to rethink how we are behaving and responding. The evergreen, 'I'm going to try harder to show you how much I enjoy being with you' and versions of this are good places to start.

Plan for success

If Child A regularly sabotages holidays, birthdays, days out and other nice times, we have to intervene. Child B has a right to enjoy their birthday, to invite their friends home and to have a day out, and Child A needs adults around them who are willing to intervene in their best interests. We won't be able to fix every situation, but some are fixable with some forward planning and trusty friends and family members. Arranging for Child A to have a day out with a family member while Child B has a birthday party can allow both to have a successful day. If you have a partner, then you can separate the children and do different activities, maybe coming together at the end of the day. Sell the arrangement in positive terms, and not, 'We're having to do it this way because you always ruin everything'. At the end of the day, express how much you enjoyed your time together. If you resent not being able to go out as a family, then this is an entirely understandable feeling. We don't enter into family life to have to take these measures. Try and remember that it won't last forever.

Change direction

Moving in the opposite direction to that which we feel driven can stir up the dynamic and, for a time, make things worse. Child A may be so used to drawing your attention through acts of violence that discovering this strategy no longer works causes them to ramp it up. The feeling of losing your attention may even be experienced by them as dangerous. One way of countering this is to offer them your attention when they are calm and satisfied with life and not when they are waving their fists. It is difficult to do this, not only because when they are calm and satisfied with life we may feel so relieved, we don't want to risk breaking the spell. Why would we, when calm is such a rare state in our households?

Giving our attention when children least expect it and under our own terms is, however, a powerful and positive way of taking control. By doing this we say: 'I am choosing to notice you', 'I experience you positively', and 'Surprise!' Good surprises, as we've looked at before, are a way of rewriting our loved one's way of interacting with us. It creates bafflement and shows that we are not as predictable and controllable as they had thought. It also is an offer of hope for change. Baffling all our children by offering our attention unbidden and unconditionally is a great strategy. It does, however, mean stepping out of the dynamic and creating a new one. One needs energy to plan and carry out this kind of manoeuvre and it becomes easier with practice.

Beware of faked evidence

On the surface, you may have a Child A and a Child B who long ago claimed their roles. Our brains like an easy summary of a difficult problem, so we end up with narratives of 'naughty child and good child', 'loud child and quiet child', 'angry child and happy child' or similar, and those narratives reinforce roles.

What if Child A often claims that Child B has done something to set them off – poked them, thrown something at them, taken something from them? You didn't notice, because the needling took place while you weren't looking. Child B is the picture of innocence. Child A is incensed and boiling. 'You never believe me,' shouts Child A. 'That's complete nonsense,' simpers Child B.

All I will say is take great care that you are seeing the situation in its entirety. Is there a chance that Child B is secretly and regularly lighting a match and throwing it into the box of fireworks, enjoying the show and then commiserating with you afterwards? Could you be complicit in this tangled and complex dynamic? I have been. Sometimes it takes someone from outside the family to see it.

You may have a Child B who does not feel safe enough to express their own trauma and expresses it through their sibling. When their sibling is starting to regulate themselves better and your home is becoming more peaceful, it may deprive them of their trauma-release valve. This may bring about ever more desperate attempts to provoke Child A, so watch out. When one child has a vested interest in the continued behaviour of another, strange things can happen. I find it best to call out these complicated twists and turns: 'Feels weird that your sister is calmer, doesn't it? Does the calm feel odd to you? I thought I noticed you winding her up', 'Maybe it's your turn to be angry now. It's fine if it is. I can manage.'

Strong and evident boundary setting

As the adult in charge of modelling assertiveness and safety we can achieve much of this by sharing out loud.

'In our home, we don't hurt people.'

'I'm keeping you safe.'

'I've got this.'

'This is what will happen next if the violence continues.'

'What happened this evening was not acceptable and there will be consequences.'

We must do this in quiet and in hectic times and communicate through our words, actions and demeanour. We may also choose to share our safety plan, or parts of it, so that our Child B knows that we have thought through our actions. If things become extremely difficult, we may need to go as far as expressing in a no-nonsense fashion, 'If this happens, I will call the police'. If you promise this, you must of course follow through.

The freedom not to accept a reparation

We talked in Chapter 14, Mopping Up and Repair, about consequences and suggested that Child A may be asked to do something nice for Child B in order to make up for a misdemeanour. When it works well, it can be an effective way of repairing. However, we must allow Child B the freedom to accept, or not, the reparation. They may feel too deeply hurt to move on, not believe in the sentiment behind the reparation, or they may be feeling bloody-minded – and why shouldn't they?

Some suggested conversation starters if you are facing such a stand-off are:

'You're not ready to accept that she is sorry and that's fine.'

'Look, your brother isn't ready yet and that's his choice. We're going to give him some time.'

Be the parent

When we are overwhelmed and don't have many people we can talk to about the realities of our lives, it can be tempting to turn to one of our children for support. However, maintaining our position in the home as parent and adult is really important because it is about being a beacon of safety and reliability and creating a home where our children can be children. This is another reason why it is essential to have someone outside our family on whom we can dump our fears, frustrations and outright fury and seek comfort from. Our children are not able to take this burden from us, even if they offer to and even if they seem to need to. Past histories of trauma may mean they have played this role before and it has a certain familiarity about it – putting their own needs in second place to keep themselves and perhaps their loved ones safe. This is not a situation we are seeking to replicate.

No secrets

Violence and secrecy so often go hand in hand. There are many complex reasons why this is the case. It is deeply shameful and shame isn't something we generally expose ourselves to by choice. Violence is outside the realm of normal experience and so we risk being hurt by the uneducated responses of others and possible exclusion from social groups. And we may fear the intervention of services.

Children living in homes where violence takes place should not be expected to keep secrets and neither should adults. Keeping secrets sends the strong message that we are not in control of the situation. Secrets also carry out half the job of manipulative and controlling behaviour. It flourishes where there is a lack of light and air.

We have set out the reasons why it is important to document the incidents in your home and to tell others about what is happening. If you and your other children are struggling then consider telling your children's teachers and other important adults in their lives what is going on: 'Her brother is struggling with violent behaviour. I want you to know because she may choose to tell you about it. We are asking for help.'

Forewarning others also allows them the opportunity to be prepared should the situation arise, and to offer help and support.

Telling a few key adults is part of our all-important safety plan. Letting all our children know that this has been done and why is an important part of our response – creating a circle of safe adults. Our children must then be given 'permission' to unburden, share and seek support. You may need to point them in the right direction: 'I'm not sure Grandpa would be as helpful to talk to as our friend. She's happy to talk to you any time you need it.'

There may be times when Child B feels great shame, for example if the police have had to visit your home. A police car, with dayglo stripes and blue lights parked outside our house, does tend to get us noticed and that attention may be extremely uncomfortable for our children. I've found that the best way of dealing with this is to acknowledge it and empathize with Child B: 'I know, it's embarrassing. I'm mortified too.'

We may help our children to make up something they can tell their friends: 'Mum lost her purse and they were returning it.'

Over time, you might be able to turn this into an almost amusing family story: 'Remember that time the police called and our nosy neighbour was listening in?'

'It's tough but we're in this together' is the sentiment we are communicating.

CHAPTER 17

Social Media

—— Sally ——

At a time when even the most well-regulated and socially accomplished adults are struggling to get to grips with the social media revolution, it doesn't bode well for our dysregulated, distressed children. Some commentators believe that this revolution is no more seismic than, say, the introduction of the printing press and we should all stop panicking. Our bet is that no one ever smashed a window or threatened their parent with a knife because they couldn't get hold of the latest pamphlet. Social media impacts on our biology in ways and at speeds that the printed word simply doesn't, and it gives children access to individuals and to information that they would never gain access to in the real world. For balance, it must be said that social media can give access to a wholesome and enriching set of experiences. For our dysregulated and vulnerable loved ones, however, it can be very far from this; in fact, for some families, social media is a curse that has brought disruption, conflict and chaos into their homes and made the already incredibly difficult job of parenting a volatile child virtually impossible.

If your child manages their use of social media well and regulates their emotions around it, then that is one great big tick in the developmental box. If the use of social media brings conflict into your home, then read on. We have brought together our personal and professional experience to try and make some sense of this brave new world and to offer some strategies that you might wish to try.

There may be a whole complicated mess of reasons why social media is catapulting our distressed young people into the Red Zone. When something is difficult to unpick, it can be enough just to gain an approximation of what's going on in order to wrestle some meaning out of the chaos. Much of what happens for our young people on social media will not be known to us, but by using the principles of threat detection, triggers, shame and attachment and some guesswork, we may be able to do some of the unravelling. When even that is beyond us, all we can do is respond to what we see.

In the BBC documentary *David Baddiel: Social Media, Anger and Us*, presenter and comedian David Baddiel reads a series of positive and negative tweets written about him, while his brain responses are monitored in a scanner. The kind, pleasant and praising tweets light up his dopamine reward network. The vile and offensive and mainly anti-semitic tweets set off his threat response, specifically the motor response relating to his hands. As Professor of Neuroscience Sophie Scott, who is running the test, explains, his hands are preparing to fight. There is a direct connection between an offensive tweet and the fight response. David Baddiel doesn't emerge from the scanner and punch a wall or a professor because he has the ability to regulate his response and to seek comfort from the other adults in the room. But even David, with his developed adult brain and his positive social networks and social capital, describes the experience of reading streams of vile tweets as 'lasting trauma'.

There is little information available about the impact of exposure to offensive, attacking and alienating posts, messages or tweets on the developing, traumatized brain but parents and carers are beginning to connect the dots. Those living on the front line of violent behaviour don't have the luxury of the time it will take to research this stuff properly (and then decide as a society what we are going to do with the results) but there is a fair amount we can reasonably assume by listening to the experiences of parents and carers and considering what we already know.

It's not too much of a stretch to assume that if vile communications create a threat response in an adult male, they will be doing at least the same to a child with an already heightened sensitivity to threat. Considering the other added difficulties our children may experience in the real world, we can begin to get an idea of how these may be playing out in the virtual one.

What might be going on?
Shame
Receiving negative comments of a personal nature or sending a message or picture that is later regretted can bring about a great big, secret shame response, especially in children with experience of neglect, abuse and loss. Shame, threat and fight are as we know, close relations.

You may witness the shame response as a parent, but have no idea where it came from and therefore little ability to offer comfort. Shame prevents young people from telling us about what just happened. And shame runs both ways – shame of receiving something hurtful and shame of sending something hurtful. Our loved one may not have behaved in an altogether honourable way either. We are dealing with children and teenagers, after all.

Social exclusion
Social exclusion is experienced in the pain centres of the brain. Social inclusion and exclusion are part and parcel of being on social media, especially for children and teens. They're pretty accomplished at falling out and ganging up against each other in the real world. The added problem with social media is that there aren't usually any adult eyes in the room and falling out can degenerate into bullying and nastiness. In short, it can all get a bit Lord of the Flies.

Missing the subtleties
Children with relational difficulties in the real world may face extra challenges in spaces where there is no access to body language, eye contact or adult assistance and mediation. Subtle cues given out in photos or messages may be missed, resulting in misunderstandings, arguments and heightened responses. Things can get out of control very quickly in the virtual (as well as the real) world. It may not take very much at all to offend, or to be offended.

Wanting to fit in and to be liked
Teenagers are very keen on fitting in with their peers. We're used to seeing this in the real world. In the virtual world, they may do some really unwise things in order to fit in and to be liked. They may get enmeshed in plans that take a long time to unravel and that ramp up anxiety and shame, or get things a bit wrong and become the subject of mockery.

Impulsivity

Sending a nude picture to a boy or a girl (or perhaps he's a 65-year-old man) you've known for five minutes, or an unkind communication to a school friend, can be down to impulsivity and not thinking through the consequences of actions. The speed of communication on social media does not allow for much consideration time, even if consideration is something your loved one might now and again manage. Again, impulsive actions can result in real-world consequences that increase stress, anxiety and the likelihood of real-world distressed responses. The shame of having posted something unwise, or of having a picture shared, has a long life – the evidence may never go away and a child's social media presence may become embedded with trauma triggers.

Dissociation or addiction?

The jury is out on whether social media is addictive in the proper sense of that word. It's fair to say that many vulnerable and not vulnerable young people struggle to regulate time spent online and can respond not very nicely when told to put down their device and eat dinner/ shower/go to bed. The big difference with many of our young people is that an enforced end to time online can result in threats, anger and violence. It may be hard for some to imagine that switching off the wi-fi, or even threatening to, could result in a child going straight into the Red Zone, but that is what many families live with. It's a very powerful response and when it comes at you it can be shocking in its immediacy and intensity.

There could be something else going on. When anything creates a bolt-out-of-the-blue fight response, survival is always at the heart of it. The thing may not appear to be anything to do with the actual business of living and may even seem silly to us, but my experience is that for our loved one, it will be a matter of survival. We've got to work really hard to see the world through their eyes.

Teens, in particular, are very concerned with belonging. Belonging, in the online space, can become something of a full-time occupation, especially for those who don't have a great sense of it in the real world. If you duck out for a while, who knows what will have happened in that time, how many conversations will have moved on and be difficult to rejoin, how many in-jokes have been shared, how many rumours have been spread. It takes a lot of hypervigilance to keep across a range of exchanges on different platforms. FOMO – or fear of missing out – is perhaps not the flippant thing we think of it as.

Time out also requires a loss of control. Some of our hypervigilant young people are not great at giving over control, because it doesn't feel safe for them. This could be another reason why our distressed young people come out all guns blazing when the wi-fi goes off.

Social media is designed to keep us well and truly hooked. Our reward networks are massaged and the little squirt of dopamine they produce when our post is liked or our tweet is retweeted or someone friends us gives us a lovely warm feeling. Could it be that the dopamine-heavy environment of social media is creating a dependency? Could coming down from dopamine be enough of a jolt to the undeveloped, distressed system to initiate the fight response? I have talked to enough parents who draw a direct parallel between social media withdrawal and drug and alcohol withdrawal to wonder if dopamine could be part of the story.

Dissociation is probably another factor we should consider and one that, if we search our own social media use deeply enough, we may have some empathy with. Shutting out the pain and struggle of the real world by diving into the virtual is something that many of us do. It's an escape of sorts, from a head full of worries. It grabs our attention and prevents our minds from wandering to who knows what dark and unsettling depths. If your child tends towards dissociation and hovers over the nuclear button when you ask them to come off their phone, you may need to think about social media, and gaming for that matter, in these terms.

Transitions

A straightforward way to think about coming on and then off social media is in terms of transitions. Children who struggle to find a sense of safety can find transitions of all sorts difficult – from leaving the park, to having a new teacher at school, to getting out of bed and embarking on the day. You may need to dust off the strategies you used to reach for to manage transitions in order to prepare your loved one for unsticking themselves from social media or gaming.

Submissive

Some of our children won't pick up their shoes without a fight, but will believe and do anything a stranger tells them online. They may lack the critical ability to question a person's identity and motives, perhaps because they really want a friend or because the strategy that kept them safe way back when was to be submissive. 'But he's my friend!' they may insist, with a lengthy explanation about how people make friends these days and how it's not like when we were young back in the dark ages. The fact that paedophiles and other criminals use the unregulated social media space to gain access to children is unlikely to cut any ice with our determined young people. Many adults also doubt that this happens in any meaningful way, perhaps because they don't ever see inside the social media spaces that children inhabit. Our social media spaces are us, including our vulnerabilities reflected back at us. A vulnerable child will leak vulnerability in all sorts of ways that flag them to those with ill-intentions.

Tribes
Young people are looking for their tribe and these days you can have access to practically any tribe or sub-tribe you want to. Aligning yourself with a tribe is an easy but simplistic way to identify yourself, stand out from the crowded crowd and gain a sense of belonging and notoriety.

Some tribes are supportive and helpful and gather around an interest, and others affirm and intensify tendencies including self-harm and anorexia, far-right views and conspiracy theories. A sense of belonging can result in a narrowing echo chamber, with no conflicting views or voices. Children who struggle to make friends in real life may be more vulnerable to blood-sucking tribes online. Some of these groups seek to seed lack of trust and conflict in adult relationships, separating children from their parents and carers. Watch out for sudden changes in behaviour and views that create conflict in your home, especially if the language used sounds as if it's come from someone else.

What can we do to keep our young people safe online and regulated, and to prevent violence from being stoked?
There is no one-size-fits-all solution in terms of keeping our young people regulated in the real and virtual world, but here are some ideas that we and others have found helpful. It's worth stating that social media and gaming use powerful psychological tools to keep their users

hooked and that being the human shield between our child and these powerful tools is incredibly hard. It's definitely a case of doing the best we can.

Keep social media off-limits for as long as possible

There will come a time when you won't be able to hold back the tide, but resisting ownership of a mobile device and access to social media can buy time for maturity to develop.

Put rules in place from the start

If your young person struggles to regulate in real life, expect the same to be true in the virtual world. Introduce rules and controls right from the start as this is much easier than trying to scrabble something together once unfettered access has become the expectation. Think about when and where access will be allowed, whether you will hold the passwords, and which apps you will allow. Start small and narrow and go from there. Bring boundaries back in if your child is struggling.

Make family spaces

Some parents keep safety around their child by having computers in family rooms only. This allows for usage to be quietly monitored and ensures an adult presence, which in itself can be regulating.

Give timed warnings

Suddenly insisting that the phone has to be put down because dinner is ready is annoying for even the most regulated of us. Give warnings for mealtimes, shower time, bedtime and time to leave for school. You will start to hate the sound of your own voice hollering: 'Ten minutes until dinner time and then phones are off' as well as the extra brain space it takes to remember to holler it, but it will have to become part of your day.

Do what works for you

Some families find that access to wi-fi before school helps to regulate their children and others find the opposite. It can either motivate children to do what they need to do, or prevent essential tasks being carried out. Bedtime is another part of the day you may need to think particularly about. Do you need to insist devices are removed at night?

Do you need to lock them away, sleep with them under your pillow or hide them in the cat bed?

Utilize the real world

It goes without saying, but our distressed children need to experience close, reliable, human relationships in order to heal and grow into healthy and socially competent individuals. Plan plenty of time out together which doesn't involve access to a phone. Get outdoors. Talk. Communicate. Play. Have fun.

Have a wi-fi-free evening

If you are struggling to stand against the might that is Silicon Valley, consider planning one evening a week when everyone in the house puts their devices aside. It is important to plan an alternative that is really attractive, such as a nice meal or a film. Make it a high point of your week and do it no matter how horrendous the week is.

Call a tech break/circuit breaker

If access to social media is playing out in the form of violence, threats, police involvement and the like then there can come a time when we have to step up and call a halt in order to keep our children and us safe from harm. This, as I am sure you will appreciate, can temporarily make matters worse.

Calling a break requires that we really step up as adults and brace against the full psychological forces that social media and gaming exert. A tech break has to be planned before it is announced and as much safety as possible must be in place when the announcement is made. It must be a serious statement of safety and care.

'Things cannot continue like this. We are stepping in. For two weeks and perhaps longer, the wi-fi is going off.' (If you begin with 'the wi-fi is going off', you may not get any further.)

'We are going to do some fun things together, because we enjoy being with you.' (It's important to sell this tech break as a positive intervention and not a show of force.)

'I know you're angry that we're stepping in.'

You may need to remove devices rather than rely on wi-fi controls, which dysregulated children can find their way around with uncanny skill.

Once the break is in place and the initial shock has settled, notice how your home feels. Children can relax into a break, begin to spend more time in family spaces and realize that they actually enjoy spending time with you. The extra opportunities for conversation and pleasant time spent together can bring about a growing sense of calm and connection, beyond just the elimination of social media. It's a virtuous circle. You may notice out loud: 'You seem calmer and happier', 'I enjoyed that conversation'. You may begin to get to know them differently. They may share things with you they may not have otherwise shared. Eventually, they may acknowledge that you were right to bring in a tech break. This has happened in my life several times, against all the odds.

Coming out of a tech break takes some skill as well. You may have bought yourself time to reconsider and redraw permanent boundaries, or to think about a wi-fi-free day. It may be best to ease out of the break, rather than to lurch back to unlimited social media use. Again, notice the changes that come with the end of the break. They will give you an indication of the extent to which social media is dysregulating your child and disrupting your family life.

Model safe social media use
It's a strategy we call on in many different guises, but modelling healthy, empowered behaviour is a quiet but powerful weapon. Sharing when someone has hurt your feelings on social media and how you are going to deal with it, or some plans for spending time offline, or even laughing at some ridiculous nonsense that has been posted somewhere can, over time, demonstrate effective strategies for life.

CHAPTER 18

School

Carly

School is often identified as a leading trigger for violence at home. It is fair to say that for the vast majority of families I work with, a massive amount of emotional energy is expended on trying to work with, fight with, support, educate and thank school staff – let alone the number of calories used in sending five hundred emails a day to do so. School is a triggering place for many children because they have so many factors that they might perceive as a threat. Secondary school is especially difficult. Children move from being in a primary environment, which is typically smaller, familiar and with fairly consistent key adults, to the secondary school, where they have a different teacher for every lesson, different lessons every day, in a different room each time. How safe they feel with key adults varies throughout the day. Work is more difficult and certain subjects get covered that could be triggering, such as sex education or discussions about death or drug use. There is so much risk-assessing going on and the smoke-detector in their brain (the threat detection system) is constantly going off. It might be helpful for us to look briefly at what, within a school day, can be a trigger. Here's a small selection:

- I'm tired.

- I have to separate from Mum and Dad.

- I have to get school transport – the kids are rowdy, and I might not know where to sit.

- I don't know who's in school today.

- It's only Monday... I've got a whole week to get through.

- I have to line up.

- I have to be first into the class.

- I need a snack, I need a snack, I need a snack.

- It's PE today.

- My teacher hates me.

- That kid I sit next to frightens me.

- I've got a test.

- I might get asked to read out loud.

- The lunch queue is bargy – there might not be any of the food I want left.

- I can't do maths.

- I might need a poo.

- My mum isn't here.

- What does he mean by that face? He doesn't like me? He's angry?

- I can't see the exit.

- I can't concentrate with all the other stuff I have to notice to stay safe.

- School is evaluative.

- My school uniform feels funny/scratchy/not right.

- I can't talk about drugs/alcohol/family relationships in personal, social and health education.

- I can't let *anyone* see I'm bad, bad, bad.

- I can't remember more than one instruction at once.

- I can only do right and wrong answers – not concepts or theories or nuance.

- I must identify and make friends with the scariest kids in school.

- I don't want *any part* of this place to be part of my home.

I'd like to give you an example of just how distressed and fearful some children can be about school. My foster daughter developed an unusual trait of leaving home for school as early as she possibly could, arriving even before several of the teaching staff. She would wait on the front part of the school property until 8.30am came around and kids could go through the gates onto the school grounds. She did this no matter what the weather. Given that she found school extremely difficult, save for a few wonderful, connective relationships with key adults she had there, this was a hugely perplexing ritual. Over several weeks and months we gently explored this with her and eventually came to understand that this was her way of getting the 'lie of the land' of the day. Seeing every staff member who arrived – who was in and who was out. Seeing every young person who arrived – who was in and who was out. This brought her a sense of control and preparation for her school day. How anxious must she have been to stand for up to an hour and a half each morning outside school? What lengths was she going to to pre-empt triggers and keep her capacity level each morning? How brave was she?

Often, children come home in the Amber Zone having held in their sense of dysregulation all day. This means they have suppressed their reactions to triggers, which means they have depleted capacity by the time they leave the school gates. Bear in mind that our children and young people don't always know, when you pick them up at 3.25pm or when they get home at 4pm, what has happened to trigger them throughout the day and wire them for home-time destruction. Once they get sight of a parent figure their attachment system is activated. What we want children to be able to do at this point is say something like 'Today was so hard, I need a hug!' but usually they cannot find the words or identify the need. Instead, they may begin to engage in some Amber Zone behaviours and it's over to us as parents to be curious, empathic and de-escalatory. Or we might read the child as being in the Green Zone, only for them to blow up over someone giving them the 'wrong' look, or they're asked to do something, or it looks as if their sibling has two more chips than them. This regular post-school dysregulation can range from apocalyptic meltdown rage to utter shutdown and relational disconnect, but whatever it is, it can leave us as parents dreading the end of the school day, putting us in the Amber Zone and sucking away the playful or breezy atmosphere that used to be your home after a day at school or work.

There is a lot of literature out there about how schools can increase children's sense of safety (I particularly recommend Rebecca Brooks' *The Trauma and Attachment Aware Classroom*[11]) but it's a battle for them to implement some of the helpful measures they read about because those in charge of school trusts or top-tier management don't buy into it. It's also challenging because targets and inspections are constantly looming and often get priority over pastoral change because of the fear of being labelled a 'bad' or 'inadequate' school.

How do we, as parents of distressed children, sometimes in collaboration with school, help our children to feel safer or shake off the dysregulation of the day in safer ways?

Where is my child at?

At the end of any school day, a couple of key skills as a parent are:

- noticing the nuances of their presentation (and reducing the demands on them when we read this as 'they've had a tricky day')

- catching their ramping-up-held-this-in-all-day anxiety (before lack of capacity sends it fight-ward).

Sometimes we can tell that they've had an onerous day because they get home, slam a door and lob their school bag across the kitchen until it lands deftly at our feet. All is clear. Other times it's a look in their eye, a redness on their face. *Very* often it's the way they try to pick a fight with us before we've drawn breath to say, 'Hello, darling. How was your...', when they ask us why we gave them cheese and onion crisps rather than salt and vinegar. To be fair, I'd hate that. Salt and vinegar all the way. It might be the glare they give their sibling that they know will provoke them into half an hour of screaming. Sometimes it's total withdrawal. Hot chocolate, sofa cuddles, going straight to the park for a run around and a snack, just a snack and/or nothing more than 'I'm really sorry you had a tough day... I'm here if you want to talk about it' are excellent remedies for this. Admittedly, that sounds simplistic but it's about you knowing what works for your child to discharge pent up energy or be soothed.

Who makes your child feel safe?

In school, it is vital that children have at least two adults with whom they feel safe, people they can contact or go to when the pangs of dys-regulation begin to rumble. Why two? Because when one is sick or on a training day, there is still another around. There is a girl I work with; I have been working with her for many years. When I first began working with her, this particular child did her absolute best to get me to dislike her. But she was so brave and funny and strong that despite her best efforts, it did not work. She is lush and very avoidant (attachment-wise). One week she and her mum came to therapy and explained, among other things, that she had been in an arduous computer science lesson and although she had asked for clarity from the teacher, she still hadn't understood the task set and had begun to dysregulate. So, she'd reached out to her pastoral support adult, Mr W via email. He was able to reply straight away. Here is how their exchange went:

April: Imannoyessir [*trans*: I'm annoyed, Sir].

Mr W: Hi April. What does that mean? Should you be doing some work?

April: Can I use my time-out card and come to you? It's just the work is so difficult and I don't get it.

Mr W: Why don't you use the time-out card and come and say hello and we'll see what we can do to help?

April: Okay.

April: Thank you [with corresponding smile emoji].

Because of the relationship that had been forged between April and Mr W, she was able to reach out to him when she recognized that she was wobbly. This was the first time at secondary school that she had been able to reach out mid-lesson in that way and, frankly, I'm tearing-up again just writing about it. This child finds school such a taxing, scary place and asking adults for help is *not* something that comes easily. But now that she has taken that brave risk of trusting one with a problem, she will be more likely to do that again.

A vicious cycle of:

Being stuck and frozen in fear = Makes a child behave in ways that reflect this = Sanctions to reinforce their badness/fear

becomes a tiny, baby virtuous one of:

> **Feeling the fear = Maybe someone can help me =**
> **They helped me = Maybe I'll try that again**

Be brave and bin it off!

An essential exercise in making school feel safer for children is reducing the pressures that come from everyday school life. School and home need to work together to decide what really matters, what our children can manage without smashing beyond their capacity and what we can bin off in terms of expectations. Here are some examples.

Assembly

Being in a crowded hall, sat on a hard floor with people in front, to the side and behind you, concentrating and not moving much. Does your child need to endure this?

Homework

I'm not sure how much primary school homework enhances learning. We all have different opinions on that. One of my children loves homework. The other three loathed it and for a couple of them it was an unnecessary battle. With secondary children, I would argue that fairly early on, we have a sense of which subjects are important or enjoyable for a child and which are not. I would look to erase any homework that feels unnecessary, freeing up the capacity of our children to be more regulated for the stuff that is important. If, like me, one of your children is unable to buy into reduced homework because they are terrified of being told off or getting into *any* form of trouble, you may wish to do the homework for them. Yep, there, I said it. And I've done it and I'm not ashamed. I'm only talking about stuff that your child has no intention of ever pursuing further and doesn't need to 'get'. For some children, just the opportunity to do homework in school will make things easier. Lots of schools have lunchtime and after-school provision for children to complete homework on the school grounds. In any case, parents and schools need to have an ongoing dialogue about this issue to keep the pressure of homework to a minimum.

Performances and Sports Day

This includes any event that means that a child will be in the spotlight, even if that's in the back row of the chorus or a line up in the egg and spoon race. If the distress caused by participating in performance is high, consider another role a child could take. Maybe they could page-turn for the pianist, make squash for the other children, be responsible for interval snacks, hold the microphone for the headteacher in between races, help the librarian, design the programme front cover. Many times, parents have chosen to keep their children off school on days when such events are taking place. That's fine but still doesn't take away the exposure to pre-performance hype in school, so giving a child a task that they will do on the day or as part of the run-up is a good idea.

Unstructured times/Playground

These times and places are the most difficult for children who do not feel ever so safe in the world and for some children who are on the autism spectrum. Anything that can be done to 'scaffold' playtime/breaktime is helpful. Clubs, supported small friendship groups, one-to-one support, giving children jobs are all things that can help. Just because other children are content to bomb around or hang around doesn't mean our children are, so giving them some structure for unstructured time is okay. When Lisa lived with us, she went through a period where unstructured times were so hard, she would come home *every* lunchtime to avoid getting into a situation that ended badly.

Maximum attendance

Children and young people who expend a large proportion of their in-school time on surviving, worrying and hypervigilance get tired. They also run out of coping-juice. When that happens, it's helpful to either give them a day off, a late morning or an early finish. Some families even need to plan a day or two off in the middle of each term to reset, reconnect and recharge.

Staying in class

When class is getting too much for our children, they need a safe place to go. This might be a safe place within the class like a tent or calm area or it might be elsewhere in school. Many secondary schools have exit rooms or exclusion rooms or sin bins where they can send disruptive children, but this reinforces their internal working models of badness. Some children will even strategize to go there because it feels better than the classroom, or they wear their frequent visits like a badge of honour. One child my son goes to school with got sent to the exit room only to return minutes later, announcing 'I got exit-ed from the exit room! Get on my level!!' More helpful are the pastoral spaces where 'it's okay not to be okay' – places where safe adults can support scared or overwhelmed children.

Other ways in which we can adapt school culture to help our children feel safe

Praise

As we've explored earlier, praise can be difficult for children who feel bad about themselves and can trigger them into flight and fight. Unfortunately, schools are places where praise is used a great deal to reward children's attainment, effort and behaviour and encourage more of the same. Because praise diametrically opposes our child's 'brittle voice' of negativity, it needs to be subtle. If a child *does* thrive on this kind of praise, great. Otherwise, please observe the following. No awards in assemblies where children come to the front of the entire class. No names on whiteboards or other public displays of praise. Please, please, *no behaviour mufti days*! I mean, why? All my children think they are dreadful. For those who don't know, 'behaviour muftis' are when any child who has had no detentions or other misdemeanours may attend school in their own clothes while all the other poor kids have to wear school uniform. Surely this is verging on abusive? And it is absolutely no incentive to behave better. When children have lost their rag or cannot face that bit of homework, the last thing on their mind is a date in the future where they won't get to wear trainers and a hoodie to school. Plus, the fact that the least attended days in schools' calendars are mufti days is evidence that they are stressful for loads of kids. Please stop them. We can still praise and award children in different ways. I'm a massive fan of praise postcards sent home, email certificates to children and quiet verbal praise, out of the limelight of a classroom. Do you remember getting handwritten letters? It was joyous. Imagine getting a postcard or letter from your headteacher or teacher saying how much they appreciate your hard work this term!

Branding children

It is easy to get into labelling children as 'violent', 'difficult', 'a runner', 'school refuser' or as 'having baggage'. The trouble with this is that it focuses on behaviour rather than their fear, worry, anxiety or dysregulation and can unconsciously feed into foregone conclusions about children rather than hope and curiosity.

Bookending the day

Children who are prone to dysregulation need help with transitioning at the beginning and end of the day. Some children need a regular hug at either end of the day. Others need to meet a key worker or eat breakfast/a snack. For children who travel a long way to school (often associated with attending specialist schools), having the opportunity to decompress from the journey and prepare for the school day is important. This might mean spending time with sensory/physical needs such as running, swinging, rocking or spinning. Children doing what they need to do at these key times in their school day can make such a difference to their sense of safety in school.

Education, Health and Care Plan

Many children in the UK with emotional stressors can have their needs documented in an Education, Health and Care Plan (EHCP). These documents serve as a record of their needs and the evidence for this. Depending on the severity or diversity of those needs, some children then benefit from funding that will allow them access to specialist schooling or teaching assistant support. These documents are about what underpins a child's behaviours. Some schools are more reticent than others to apply for EHCPs as the process is somewhat arduous, but parents can also apply for these (it's still arduous but another way to skin a metaphorical cat). There is a risk that if children's needs are not clearly defined and evidenced in such a document, they end up in provisions that are totally unsuitable, particularly if they are permanently excluded from school.

I'll check that out!

Children with trauma often like to keep adults in their lives away from each other because the more they do this, the more they have a shot at staying in control. It is immensely helpful if adults check with one another what they have been told by children. So, if a child comes to you as a school staff member and says, 'My sister is going into care' or says to you as a parent, 'Mr Black said I didn't need to do his homework any more', feel free to deploy the *accept and check* rule: 'Oh, thank you for telling me. I'll check that out with your mum/teacher.'

Children aren't always deliberate in their exaggeration of the truth. Sometimes it's a matter of survival and entirely subconscious. Checking out doesn't need to be triggering for a child, rather a matter-of-fact way of life.

No double punishing

We've all heard the phrase, 'What happens in Vegas stays in Vegas'. I put it to you that, 'What happens in school stays in school'. As parents, it's important that we support the school's methods of asserting boundaries (unless those are unreasonable or massively unhelpful). However, we do not need to add to these at home. If our child has a detention for disrupting class or their peg has been on a stormy cloud all day, we do not need to exercise further sanctions or consequences at home. Home needs to be the safe zone. Admittedly, if your child, like mine, smashes a glass pane at school then sure, we need to address this and think about repair. Thinking about repair and helping our child *do* repair are parts of our therapeutic parenting but if that has already been covered by school then leave it alone. Let your child know that they had a hard day and that you're there if you want to talk about it. It's *always* important that they know we know what's happened and *sometimes* important to talk it through. The relationship our child has with us as parents is the most important one they have. We need to preserve this and avoiding double punishment is one way of doing that.

Choosing a school

This is something I get asked about a lot and it is something of a minefield. Some parents go for a small village-type school to ensure that their child isn't overwhelmed by a large school, only to find that no adults at that school have ever considered 'trauma' or how that is expressed in a child, and your kid is the one sticking out like a sore thumb and considered a scourge by all the other parents. Some parents send their children to schools where there are loads of kids who have or who are experiencing significant relational trauma and staff are well versed and warm-hearted in responding to such difficulties. However, it can be the case that your child is triggered by so much drama when there are other traumatized children in the classroom.

Here are a few questions you might want to ask or provisions you might want to seek out when choosing a school:

- What training has the school had on attachment and trauma and when did this take place?

- Where would my child go to dysregulate and is that place nurturing or shaming?

- What are the school's behavioural policies and how are they conveyed to children? How individualized or flexible are these?

- What provision is there for unstructured times, such as nurture groups, buddies, clubs or staff organizing specific activities?

- Does a child's Pupil Premium (Plus)* get used specifically for your child or absorbed into a general special educational needs budget?

- How will the school seek to provide your child with two 'safe' key adults and how will those relationships be formed? How does the school support transitions from year to year and term to term?

---

*   A fund used to increase educational outcomes for disadvantaged children. It includes all children eligible for free school meals, children looked after (in the case system) or children previously looked after.

Relationship, relationship, relationship

There are many dedicated school staff who go the extra mile for children and young people with complexities to meet their needs and increase their sense of safety. Some staff are pastoral-hearted and do this quite naturally. Others learn it. Either way, these wonderful humans have sensed the need in these children and taken the time and patience to get to know them, understand the theoretical world behind their tricky behaviours and how best to support them. I should also tip my invisible hat and buy a metaphorical pint for those who do this for the children who present as '*fine*' in school – compliant, helpful, studious, hardworking and quiet. They are the staff who believe us as parents when we say of such a child, 'I think they mask a great deal of anxiety in school, and we get the aggressive fallout at home.' If that is you reading this now, thank you. Thank you. Oh, thank you.

But then there are other school staff who do not 'get it' – either because they don't know about trauma/attachment/capacity/flight-fight-freeze, or because they don't believe in it (it's all woolly, liberal mumbo-jumbo) or because they don't care. Let me be clear and, I would argue, fair. Teachers are not therapists. They are not our child's parent, either. Their role in our child's life is different and they went into teaching to become teachers. Teachers do not arrive on their first day at work expecting to be told 'Welcome! Now go and be a therapist to that bunch of kids over there. Yes, those ones there who will do nothing you say, will disrupt your class, make other children cry, *demand all your attention, all of the time*, sit under tables, make your attainment target mean plummet, and call you a c**t.' Teachers do not expect this any more than I expect to turn up to work to find a room full of children needing me to teach them maths (which would result in panic, thrusting me into freeze).

Several of my besties are teachers or teaching assistants and they went into the job to teach because they enjoy hanging out with children or young people and want to inspire them to get excited about their subject and to achieve their potential in any way. But that is still a step removed from connecting with a child's internal pain and fears. One of my friends can even recall the moment he decided to be a teacher. He was using a jumper to help a child learn to ride a bike, training their eyes to look ahead and not down, like a bull fighter but much gentler and without the frilly clothing and tan. The sense of achievement, warmth and modest pride he felt about teaching that child to learn to ride a bike was one he wanted to feel again as a teacher, and I'm happy to report that he is a wonderful teacher.

Trauma has a powerful knack of making us feel useless because it feels as if we can't do our jobs, whether that's as a parent or a teacher. Teaching is an extremely demanding, pressurized job. During Covid pandemic times, one could add the work 'gruelling' to that description. I. Could. Not. Do. It. Whenever we begin a new career, we have certain hopes and expectations. Sometimes we have an open heart to learn and be curious. Sometimes we manage our own sense of safety by stoically clinging on to control. Sometimes we're a bit of both. I guess the former is more helpful if that career involves providing something for other people. I make this point because, irrespective of where a school member of staff sits on the mega control-completely open continuum, relationships between children and adults in school are key – key to their learning, key to their regulation and key to their sense of safety.

It is worth noting at this point that it isn't just frontline school staff who are part of how safe a child feels. Sometimes it's that wonderful receptionist who always greets the child with a smile and a welcoming tone, or the lunchtime assistant who walks around the playground, hand in hand with our kid talking endlessly about their shared love of dogs.

In our roles as therapeutic parents, we became accustomed to communicating on a daily basis with key members of our kids' school team. If our kid left home upset, off an email would go. I remember getting a reply after I sent an email following a tricky morning at home (because of whatever was perceptually about to happen in school). The reply said, 'Thank you. Forewarned is forearmed'. No shit. That level of communication saw my kid make it through to leavers' day in Year 11. The staff member I sent it to was Mr A, of 'Goongate' mentioned in Chapter 3. Mr A was a games teacher at the time of Goongate. Games was a particularly difficult lesson for Lisa because it involved getting changed, competition and being exposed (remember lining up to take your turn at a long jump, netball shot or penalty? Hideous). Those were enough to harmfully diminish her capacity and make her red-faced. And then, that day, something went wrong on the playing field. I don't remember what. The unsuspecting Mr A tried to correct Lisa in some way, and it finished off the nub of regulatory capacity that she had left. She left the sports field yelling that he was a 'F**king goon'. Rather than taking this at face value, Mr A became curious about this kid and what it was about her that she found games so difficult. He was curious with us and open-minded and warm with Lisa. Unsurprisingly, Mr A became one of two key members of staff that saw her through school. They were her safe adults. Mr A was promoted to pastoral wings of the senior leadership team and some years later in this role, he and I were reflecting on that first encounter he had with Lisa. He was gracious enough to say, 'Yeah, I picked a fight with Lisa that day and she won.'

When Lisa arrived on the back of a motorbike for her leavers' day in Year 11, she hadn't been in our care for about nine months. I went along to cheer her on, as did her former youth leader from a church group she attended. As you might imagine, I was in tears, both overjoyed that she had finished school and could celebrate that like any other child but also incredibly sad that she was no longer living with us. Mr A was there too. He spotted me in my snivelling state and gave me a hug. Forging supportive relationships with people who also look after our children is a must if we are to best provide the right school experience our children deserve.

CHAPTER 19

Threats to Safety from Family Members

Carly

This chapter discusses the perils and predicaments we face when our children's sense of safety is undermined or threatened by other family members. For children living with an adoptive or foster family or those with a Special Guardianship Order* (SGO; also called kinship care), this might be any form of contact they have with their birth parents or even birth siblings, whether it be face to face, by letter or via social media. There is also a whopping number of birth parents caring for their birth kids who must grapple, manage and soothe the effect that the behaviour of the *other* parent has on their child(ren). It is well documented that in some domestic abuse situations, when the injured party breaks free from their abusive partner, that abuse continues through their children.[12,13,14] These are the cases that get dragged through the family courts, often over and over again, because there isn't enough evidence that the abusing parent is emotionally terrorizing the child, but the overwhelming experience of the non-abusing parent is that it's utterly rife. These are the children who get asked/told by social workers, guardians and well-meaning teaching staff:

'Why are you so angry with Mummy/Daddy?'

'What sorts of things do you enjoy doing with Mummy/Daddy?'

---

* Special Guardianship Orders offer permanence to children's living arrangements in the form of awarding authority for their care to family members or significant others such as an auntie or grandparent.

'Is there anything that Mummy/Daddy says or does to make you worried?'

'Does Mummy/Daddy talk about Daddy/Mummy?'

'You shouldn't hit your Mummy/Daddy.'

'What else could you do instead of hitting?'

In terms of understanding what is going on or even being able to help these children, this can reach an impossible position. I have worked with multiple families with non-abusive (formerly known as the domestic abuse victim) parents and their children, only to have the work shut down because the abusive parent frightens the child about talking to anyone about what is said or done while the child is with them. These children go into school and therapy paralyzed by the fear that they will say something they should not. So, this chapter applies to all those children too, who have conflicting yet compelling relationships with their birth family. For the rest of this chapter, I will refer to these families as previous domestic abuse families.

I'd also like to mention those families (SGO/Kinship) caring for children of their own family – grandparents, aunties, uncles, step-parents, and so on. In these cases, it is highly likely that the children you look after were not 'sought out' by you as such but came to your home because of some difficulty in your wider family and you did the 'right thing'. Perhaps you're reading this book because you regret doing so because it's bloody hard (understatement) and you never expected to be spending your forties/fifties/sixties in this position. You had other plans, but you committed to the child(ren) you took on, and the influences, choices and behaviours of their birth parents (in whatever form these may take) are a complicating factor in the mix. A ball ache. A fly in the ointment. One less thing you could do without.

Losing or being displaced from members of our birth family is painful and complicated, irrespective of whether we are five minutes or 55 years old. We feel loss, anger, grief, regret, blame, confusion. Many of us are familiar with Kübler-Ross's[15] Stages of Grief that are denial, anger, bargaining, depression and acceptance. I would argue that three of those stages – anger, bargaining and acceptance – are more difficult to work through and somehow prolonged if we have had no regular contact with a parent/sibling we have lost for years. And Kübler-Ross's model is about death rather than removal or displacement, but I think the stages are still relevant. They just have a tricky twist and rarely progressed through sequentially.

Let's talk about some of the attitudes towards their birth parents that children who have been fostered, adopted or separated from their birth families, or those children from previous domestic abuse families, might hold.

The fantasied angels

Some children will imagine that their birth parents were like Rapunzel's or Sleeping Beauty's parents, that they were snatched or hidden away from their loving parents, leaving them behind and bereft. Such children dream of the day they can be reunited with their first parental loves. It's not necessarily as dramatic as that but even degrees of this can complicate things. Please do not misunderstand me. Often, birth parents love and adore their children but do not have the capacity to take care of them. Where that story is true, the story must be told. Where it wavers from this in some way (or in an enormous way), the story must be told. The most worrying aspect of the fantasied angels complex is that it has the potential for children to avoid fully connecting with their 'growing-up' families or thinking that they are liars, in the case of children from previous domestic abuse families.

The I-need-to-rescue-them

Knowing that your parents were/are homeless, addicted to substances or potentially dead is frightening. This is a powerfully constant worry for many children who do not live with birth parents. One child was brave enough to tell their safe adult that they wished their birth parent would die because they knew they were going to and then they would be able to stop worrying about it. That might sound awful, but in the context of that scenario, the child was absolutely right, their parent was likely to die, and they did. If, as a child, you have seen your birth parent comatose on the sofa for days on end in a 'death-like' state, you quickly get organized about whether that person is alive or dead. Or if your social worker, try as they might, is unable to locate your birth parent because they are so off the radar for months or years, it's a fairly normal response to carry a knot in your stomach. In terms of distress-fuelled violence, this isn't always the root cause but sometimes it just flares up when the weather is cold, or on birthdays or some other trigger. For children from previous domestic abuse families, it might be that they are regularly fed the line that the abusive birth parent is horribly affected by the actions of the safe parent, that the safe parent is telling lies about them, that they would end their life if they could not regularly see their children. Emotional stone around your neck, anyone?

The why-couldn't-you-look-after-me-too?

If your birth parents have been unable to look after you but then gone on to have more children that they *have* been able to parent safely (or more safely), it's something of a slap in the face, which sometimes translates as a slap in ours. It just exacerbates their already shitty internal working model and is utterly confusing. It can feel to the child like being replaced by a better, newer model, as we might do with a software update, phone or car. But worse, because they're a human, not a thing.

The I-want-to-hurt-you-but-I-can't

I have worked with adolescents who have experienced significant abuse in their early childhoods. Consequently, some have feelings of anger and rage towards their abusers, and thoughts about enacting physical violence on them. Some clearly imagine specific acts of violence and a few talk about those with me. Usually they tell me quietly, with no amount of bravado and can feel ashamed or afraid of where their thoughts take them. But these young people aren't able to even *tell* their abusers what they think, let alone take physical revenge. So where does the energy go, the energy that gets stored up inside, wanting to say or do what they feel they need to? Their families – those who take care of them day to day. We often bear the brunt for words unspoken or acts unfulfilled (some of which we're jolly glad are not fulfilled) because our poor kids are left impotent to express this directly to those to whom their anger belongs.

The I-was-too-bad-for-you

Many children I work with grow up with a fundamental belief that their behaviour and 'badness' were too much for their parents to manage and that this is the reason why alternative care was found for them or why a parent left. Such a view is carried around by children within their time in their safe family and can interfere with their connections in safe families, believing themselves unworthy of love and care. Furthermore, when episodes of violence or aggression occur, it reinforces this view of themselves: 'I was too bad then and I'm too bad now.' Just carrying around this message makes them more predisposed to distressed-fuelled violence because violence is great at proving your unconscious point.

The I-am-terrified-of-you or of-turning-into-you

Children can fear turning out like their parents – in prison, harmful, addicted. When their distress manifests in violence, this starts to feels like a self-fulfilling prophecy and it's important that we, as parents, carers and professionals, gently remind children that it is not a foregone conclusion that their parent's story will be theirs. In the case of adopted and fostered children who have had complicated life journeys, this highlights the importance of undertaking brilliant quality therapeutic life story work with them. Such work seeks to dispel the myths that children have been told or ones they have come to hold themselves about their earlier lives and how they sit in the family arrangement.

Children can move between these models of their (birth) families as they grow up and can hold multiple models at any one time. Whatever model(s) they hold, *not knowing* is so powerful – over and above the model that you provide for them. Therefore, it is likely that the draw to birth families is present in some way (ranging from ever so tiny to extremely powerful). What does this have to do with distress and violence? Hmmm, a lot, if your child gets overwhelmed by any of their thoughts and feelings regarding their birth family. As I've already said, I have worked with several young people who have told me how they would like to punish their abusers or grow up to be vigilantes or torturers. Some children/young people are triggered by physiological or neurological aftershocks of their time in their birth families. I have known many young people who prolifically use drugs/alcohol, engage in risky behaviour or drama because their bodies remember the sensation of this and remain drawn to it. Some children understand that their procedural or learning difficulties are a direct result of their parent's lifestyle, treatment of them or conduct while that child was in-utero.

Family time and forms of contact

When children are placed for adoption or into care or with extended family members, contact of any kind with birth families can bring with it a shopping trolley full of sensitive goods all labelled *highly fragile*. Mixed loyalty is a common one, as is a child's sense of reality being undermined. They might say something along the lines of, 'I experience my mum as good and caring but my gran/dad/aunt says that she is a vindictive witch... Am I crazy? Who do I listen to? Did my mum really do/say that thing?' As a child, someone telling you that your reality isn't real, particularly about someone you love, has a potential effect on your mental health that could be devastating and manifest in self-hatred and aggression. I've seen it and it's so ugly. Here are some other specific types of contact that can bring distress to our child and our homes.

Direct contact

For those of our children who have face-to-face contact with members of their birth family, we often have to bookend the waiting game and the aftermath with truck-loads of down time or distraction or regulation, regulation, regulation. Even when that contact is mainly positive, the intensity of only seeing those family members once/twice/thrice per year sets in motion a mixture of anxious and excited anticipation in our children. If you are a foster parent or parent of a child from a previous domestic abuse family, it's likely that this direct contact will be more frequent, and you will need to manage dysregulation ranging from incessant talking to bed-wetting to distressed violence every time such an event is scheduled. Often birth parents struggle themselves to know how to 'be' with their children, or the child goes into demanding or bullying mode to elicit gifts or money. One such child I helped to support in residential care did exactly that. I thought with his residential adult team about how we could improve family time and we concluded that part of the difficulty was that the parent had no idea about how to connect to him and vice versa so they both ended up falling back on old ways of being with one another. Where connection is awkward or clunky, it can help to 'restrict' family time to a supported, shared and structured activity, such as bowling or cinema or crazy golf and maybe some food afterwards. This might seem superficial, and, in some ways, it is, because it's pitched at the level that both parties can emotionally handle. It has worked really well for children and their parents, especially where there are others around who can emotionally 'hold' the child and parent and be clear about the boundaries during their time together. It's also more connecting than the parent and child sitting in a park for an hour with both parties unsure about what to say or do, or, worse, either of them reverting to unhelpful or abusive ways of being with one another. Where close monitoring is needed for safety, building in lots of structure and 'small wins' is key to success.

Direct time with birth families may also induce fear in children because, well, they're scared of their birth families. When they've had to hold in that fear, one can't help being surprised if that gets discharged before and after their family time in ways that are aggressive or violent. It might be that we must work very hard at noticing that out loud, giving it narrative and blanketing it with empathy:

> 'I've noticed things get really tricky around here after you've seen your mum.'

> 'You seem really angry every time you're due to see Dad. I wonder if there's a lot of worry behind that anger...'

> 'I know that the next few days will be rough because you're seeing your siblings. I'm here if you need me and I'll stay close so I can keep you safe.'

Sometimes the effect of direct time with birth families is so challenging for children that changes and reductions are necessary. It's important to be very clear with children and parents about *why* those changes are being made and *who* is making that decision.

Letterbox exchanges

In the context of adoptive families, it is common for children and birth parents to exchange one or two letters per year via a Social Services department. These letters have specific times of the year that they are sent. Such practices are also possible with kinship fostering situations but less common than they are in adoption. These letters can be difficult for children to read or hear because they remind them of their early life experiences. Equally, when letters don't get sent from birth parents, this runs the risk of children going into worry-mode about them. Some children want to avoid reading or hearing the letters and others are angry about them because they do not acknowledge the harm the child(ren) suffered while in the care of birth parents. It's not all doom and gloom because such practices can reassure children that they are remembered by their birth family and that the birth family is alive.

Online contact

By far the most difficult form of contact to navigate is online because we, as parents, have such little influence over the boundaries of the contact and it can escalate very rapidly. Many parents and carers have come to understand that it is crucial to convey to our children that when they want to start making connections with birth families, they will be openly supported. No secrets, no fears. It's a natural desire to know where we have come from, and many parents want to be *alongside* their children when that happens. Despite all the best intentions from parents and carers, online contact can spiral into something intense and akin to a runaway train. Birth siblings can convince children that their known story is all a lie, and their birth parents were screwed over by Social Services. Some children arrange meet-ups with their birth families unbeknown to their adoptive/kinship/foster families. This can go a few ways. Either children are freaked out by the values/lifestyles/intensity of birth families and head right back to the safety of home. Or they are excited/attracted/drawn to them, and it can generate cut-ties or rejection of the family they grew up in. This scenario is many adoptive families' worst nightmare. It can be that the child's 'itch' about their birth family gets satisfactorily scratched and it's just enough to be in touch with them from time to time in a laid-back sort of way.

PART 5

Take Care of Yourself and Travel in Hope

CHAPTER 20

Take Care of Yourself

─── Sally ───

This part of our book isn't about your child and their struggles and needs and how you must bend and shape yourself to care for them, it is about you and your needs. This is also the part of our book where you probably want to reach out, grab us by the arms and tell us how impossible it is to find the time, energy or opportunity to take care of yourself. You may also be tempted to skip this chapter. Please don't. There is always a mountain of compelling reasons why you absolutely cannot take care of yourself. I'm going to try and convince you of the mountain of compelling reasons why you should and must take care of yourself and suggest some ways to start doing that.

For a long time now, your child and their violent behaviour will have swallowed up your life and quite possibly brought you to your knees. It seems impossible, and even unsafe, to turn your attention anywhere else, let alone towards your own needs and so you march on, taking each day as it comes, relentlessly doing your best and wishing for a time when life doesn't have to be like this.

I have met many parents and carers who have struggled under these conditions and not one of them has ever said: 'I wish I'd taken less care of myself'. I've met plenty who have learned the hard way that unless they master the art of topping up their reserves and preserving their sense of themselves, things can unravel very quickly. Regular repair work goes towards preventing catastrophe and is cheaper in the long run. Think of it as an investment, in your family, in you and in your future.

If you have ever been floored by the reality of parenting in the face of violence, you will know how hard it is to recover. Empty tanks take a lot of refilling. I used to imagine there were holes in mine, where the energy I thought I'd saved just poured away. It took me years to truly replenish my reserves. I know many parents who have had the same experience and who have had to take the business of recovery and self-care extremely seriously.

Taking care of ourselves – the approaches we take and what works for us – is highly personal and too much specific advice can be counter-productive. I've read many advice columns such as 'Ten Ways to Nurture Yourself' and been left feeling worse than ever. I couldn't muster up the strength required to 'Ring a friend and invite them out for coffee!' or 'Plan a trip to the theatre!' even if I'd wanted to. I must also mention a whole-body repulsion I developed at the thought of spa days and treatments. I think it was about the vulnerability of being semi-naked around strangers and having to lower the barricades I'd erected around my personal space. Self-care has to be tailored and no more so than for those living with threats to their safety.

I've set out some self-care approaches that have worked for me. I've learned a lot of this from the therapists who have helped me through, and some from hard experience. Looking back from a position of relative peace, I can report that nurturing myself in order to be a better parent and a happier person took me a long time to master but was an essential piece of the puzzle.

Reconnect with your body

If you find yourself existing mainly inside your head, or your physical self has shrunk and collapsed in on itself, get back inside that body. I did this through walking, running, stamping and stretching. Getting out into the fresh air, feeling the breeze on my face and smelling the outside world planted me back in the real world and re-centred me. Moving around to music helped me, too.

Remember who you are

Have you lost sight of yourself? What are your talents and interests? What were your hobbies before they got squeezed out of your life? What are your quirks? What makes you, you? Think about her/him. Does she/he need to make a return? When we live in fear, it can feel dangerous to reveal ourselves in all our wonderful complexity, but it is only as complete people that we can hope to steer our families back to safety and equilibrium.

Put down your tools

Are you slugging away at a problem? Stop, at least for a while. Have a rest. Hear the silence. Remind yourself of the choices you have. What's the worst that could happen if you downed tools for a while? It's a hard lesson for some of us to learn, but fixing is not the answer to everything.

Ask yourself a question

A therapist, to whom I owe a great deal, taught me that at a decision point, when you are about to get dragged into a situation, you should ask yourself this: 'But what do I need?' I've found it an effective way of stopping me in my tracks and forcing me to think about my choices. It injects a moment of stillness into a loud, fast, chaotic string of events. What I've learned is that some times, choosing to either intervene or not intervene in a situation makes no difference to the eventual outcome.

Take a break

If you live in a house filled with trauma, you absolutely have to get away from it from time to time. There will be a heap of reasons forming in your mind as to why you cannot escape, even for an hour. They may be valid, but I can only report that listening to those reasons didn't work for me in the long term. I had to train myself to turn the question around – what would I need to do in order to get away for an hour? The necessity of your time off becomes the problem to solve.

If the answer to the problem is, we have to ask someone to sit in our home and watch our child while we go to a café, or for a walk, again we will be thinking up all the possible catastrophes that may ensue. Cease the catastrophic thinking. If the arrangement fails, then it fails, but you tried and you may have learned how to make it work next time. If it wasn't a great success, but nothing dreadful happened, then take it as a win and do it again. If it worked well, then go for it. What you absolutely must do for that hour though, is not worry. Easier said than done I know, but worrying never changed anything, ever, but it has ruined lots of good times.

When we can build our tolerance to taking breaks and accepting the support we need to make them happen, we should aim higher – half a day, a day, a weekend. If you can achieve these dizzy heights then everyone in your life, including your distressed child, benefits. Taking a break is for the greater good.

Ask for help

If we're lucky we have people in our lives who say: 'Let me know if you need anything'. The problem is, we rarely do. There are many barriers, including wondering if they really meant it and coming up with something useful and practical that would make a difference. I've found that approaching our friends and loved ones with a specific and time-limited request can unlock support.

'Could you watch her for an hour while I go for a walk?'

'Could you cook for us once a week?'

Diet

I won't dwell on this, but crisps, chocolate, ice-cream, alcohol, pizza, chips and other processed crud are a great one-off response to a horrendous day, but they are not the fuel of champions. As Olympic parents and carers, we must fuel ourselves as such. As well as requiring solid and sustainable amounts of energy, you are also living with incredible levels of stress. I've followed the developing research on the effects of prolonged stress and inflammation on the body and let's just say it's not great. Diet and exercise are possibly our most effective weapons against it.

I want to leave you with a thought about your future self because they don't often get a look in when we live minute-by-minute. Who is that person? What incredible things has she/he survived and achieved? What does she/he do with her/his time? Our future selves deserve to enjoy their lives as whole, healthy people, having carried out such sterling work for the good of others. Take a few steps towards that person and fill in some of the detail, love and nurture them and bring them into being.

CHAPTER 21

Travel in Hope

Sally

Raising the next generation and equipping them for life is the most important and yet least valued role in our society. Those raising children who have lived through difficult times and who express their distress through violence are not only undervalued, they are isolated, misunderstood, starved of support and excluded from services. It's a really shitty hand to be dealt.

This book is our effort to add to the sparse writing and support for parents and carers living with violence. We hope it has been encouraging, empowering and of real help to you. We have intentionally approached the subject as something of an imperfect mix of art and science because we strongly believe that's what it is. There is no 'one-size-fits-all' and that's why it's important to try out a variety of strategies and find out what works for you, always remembering that what works on a Tuesday may not work on a Wednesday. It's a style of parenting that demands flexible and creative thinking, compassion and self-compassion.

The thought I'd like to leave you with is this – you may be walking an extremely treacherous and steep road and you may doubt your ability to continue on, but by taking each day as it comes and by slowly equipping yourself and your loved one with skills and knowledge, the road will gradually become a little easier. There will come a day when you no longer have to parent in the face of such immense distress, and sometimes that hope is all you may have to hang on to. You may not yet be able to imagine that day, but it will come.

I wish you all the luck, and the very best hiking boots.

—— Carly ——

As the therapist in our bumbling duo, I find myself wondering where you have landed at the conclusion of this book. Are you relieved to know that you're not alone and there are immediate quick-wins, as well as longer-term interventions you can do, or have you already started these with your child? Are you surprised or disappointed about how much of responding to your child's aggression is about changes you need to make? Are you sad, empowered, determined, connected? Let me tell you where I am. I am remembering the day that Lisa left and the pain I felt. I remember every second of it. I also remember those people who were right there next to us, as they had been the day she arrived. I feel a sense of enormous sadness and loss for those of you who do not have that network of incredible supporters and I pray that you and those around you will find a way to change that place of loneliness and isolation. I remember the day we saw her again, the day she chose to come back into not just our lives, but the lives of her extended family, the people who loved her and us through it all. No, it's not a Disney film and she never moved back in. But she didn't let us go again either. She had to reach the depths of shitville before she was ready (multiple times, I think) but she made it back and, more importantly, we found a sustainable way of being her family. I have to say this next sentence otherwise she'll never forgive me. She was and *is* a pain in the arse. But she's our pain in the arse.

Sometimes there needs to be a parting of ways before we and our child can reconnect in safer ways. That has been the experience for both Sally and me. Other times, it's non-shamingly 'outing' the violence, reviewing boundaries, allowing natural consequences to take their course or our supporting network getting more helpfully involved with our lives that stop or minimize violence. Recently I was talking with a parent about the potential scenario she is facing of having to give evidence against her son, whom she loves dearly, about violence committed against her. When we live with distressed violence and aggression, we find ourselves contemplating situations we never thought we would be in. Yet, also as part of that discussion, we talked about the evidence we had seen about how much healthier their relationship was since living separately and how the lad had shown signs of independence skills she did not know he had. This world is full of contradictions, twists and turns. We find ourselves discovering capacities and superpowers that previously lay dormant or undiscovered. Sure, we'd much rather they were discovered while doing the shopping or going for a run, but it doesn't work like that. The power of our remaining emotional availability to a child whose behaviour makes that a risky choice is difficult and wonderful, and we truly hope that some parts of this book have aided you in holding on to that choice.

Appendices

Appendix A: Window of Tolerance Model

In the main part of the book, we talk about *capacity*. This idea is based on something known as the Window of Tolerance, which is a theory of Dan Siegel's[16] (1999). The Window of Tolerance Model helps us to understand how we manage calm, stress and overwhelm at any given moment. Here is a diagram of what the Window of Tolerance model looks like.

Window of Tolerance Model

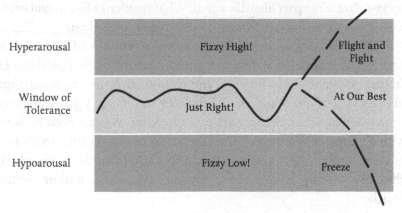

When we are pushed beyond our Window of Tolerance our 'arousal' level operates outside our ability to rationalize, problem-solve or collaborate in regulated ways. We either go into *hyperarousal*, which is a mobilized physical state or *hypoarousal*, which is a demobilized physical state. And sometimes we go into hyperarousal before crashing into hypoarousal. Imagine that the hormones involved in these processes are like a car, specifically that those relating to hyperarousal are the accelerator and those relating to hypoarousal are the brakes. When our sense of safety is compromised, biologically speaking, we cope by means of *flight, fight* or *freeze*. In flight and fight, this involves increased heart rate, sensitivity to *any* additional forms of threat or negativity, and cortisol and adrenaline being released into the blood stream. Cortisol is a hormone that manages our glucose for when we need it most, especially during stress because we need much more of it when we're in that state. It also shuts down functions that get in the way of threat or stress management such as digestion, immunity and reproductive systems. No one needs those in a time of certain crisis, right? Adrenaline kick-starts all the bodily functions we need to run or fight such as increased heart rate, blood pressure, expanding air passages in our lungs and sending blood to the muscles we need the most. In freeze, acetylcholine acts as a brake to the accelerator, slowing down the heart rate and allowing the body to be restored to regular functioning. However, if our bodies get flooded with acetylcholine, it's like brakes getting slammed on too hard and we crash through the windscreen and land immovable somewhere on the bonnet or the ground (apologies American readers, I hope you're managing the trans-Atlantic car part identification). What that looks like in real life is feeling low or depressed, frozen, dissociated or 'spaced out'.

The interesting and *vital* thing about the Window of Tolerance is that it isn't static. It narrows and widens according to a plethora of factors, physical, environmental and emotional. Sometimes a change in the width of our Window of Tolerance can happen gradually over time whereas other changes are more fleeting. We can even be born with a narrower Window of Tolerance if exposed over time to trauma of some kind in-utero. Let's re-read a scenario from the book, which although made up, happens every day across the world in some version or other:

> *It's Monday morning and seven-year-old Josie is in foster care. She is in foster care because of serious neglect and exposure to domestic and substance abuse. At the weekend, her birth parent didn't show up for the monthly contact they have and she doesn't know why. Josie finds school difficult and the first part of today is maths – her least favourite subject and one she is way behind her peers with. She manages to get through maths and it's breaktime. She plays with her best friend outside and when they come back in for snack*

time, the only fruit left is a banana, which she absolutely hates. The rest of the morning goes well, although by lunchtime she is very hungry. She runs to get to the front of the lunch queue and is told off for doing so and sent to the back of the line. She eventually gets to eat her food, which she wolfs down to get outside to play before her friend starts playing with someone else. In the afternoon, there is a supply teacher as her own teacher has gone on some training. Josie is very quiet because she doesn't know this teacher and the topic is 'families'. Josie gets told off for fidgeting and later the teacher picks her out to share with the class something about her family. Josie remains silent and so the teacher asks her again. When Josie remains quiet, another child volunteers out loud, 'She hasn't got a mummy'. Josie leaps from her chair, screams an obscenity at the child then flees the classroom, knocking over pencil boxes, books and display work as she leaves.

Okay, now let's track Josie's Window of Tolerance and what triggers there were that pushed her outside this. Factors that *narrowed* Josie's Window of Tolerance were:

- her early history of neglect and domestic violence

- cancelled contact

- hunger

- supply teacher.

The triggers and where these put Josie in her Window of Tolerance were:

- Monday morning and maths (hypoarousal)

- breaktime (inside Window of Tolerance)

- no snack left (back into hypoarousal)

- running to lunch (hyperarousal)

- being told off, sent to back of queue and eating quickly (hyperarousal)

- supply teacher and topic of families (hypoarousal)

- being told off for fidgeting and asked to share with class (hyperarousal)

- another child saying she doesn't have a mummy (hyperarousal).

Within Josie's brain (and ours) there are two important parts associated with the journey I have described. The first is the hippocampus, which is critical to our ability to emotionally regulate and could be viewed as the width of our Window of Tolerance at any given moment. The second is the threat detection system, which as well as being a potentially high-scoring word in Scrabble, is responsible for sounding the threat/danger alarm. It assesses *every* stimulus it detects as safe or unsafe. Anything unsafe becomes a trigger for a change in where we are in our Window of Tolerance. An understanding of what influences our children's Windows of Tolerance enables us to create environments that expand their Windows while avoiding triggers. If they're inside their Window of Tolerance, we can expect more thinking, rationale, capacity and regulation from them. If they are outside it, we cannot and we therefore adjust our expectations, demands and parenting accordingly. If our children understand this too, it can help them to plan for situations where their tolerance will be narrowed. It also helps us to assess our own Window of Tolerance, a vital tool in therapeutic parenting.

Appendix B: The Polyvagal Ladder

The Polyvagal Ladder[17] helps us to think about where we or our children are in our nervous systems – our states. How our bodies need to interact with the world depends on what is required of them and includes how safe we perceive it to be in any given moment. The sympathetic branch of our nervous system is the mobilized, activating part. It gets us out of bed in the morning, gives us those butterflies or fast beating heart when we're about to perform or take an exam. It also sends us into *flight* and *fight* when we detect danger. The parasympathetic branch of our nervous system is designed for rest, digestion and bodily repair/replenishment and for *freeze* (defensive shutdown). Polyvagal theory posits a secondary branch of the parasympathetic system that allows us to function within our social engagement system but it only does so when we feel safe. Polyvagal theory is thought about like a ladder.

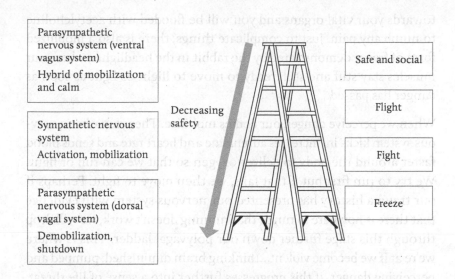

Let's start at the top and work our way down the ladder. To do this we're going to take a walk in the woods.

Safe and social: Imagine you are taking a walk in some beautiful woods with some family or friends. You will be able to talk, plan for the past, reflect on the future. You can laugh or talk about trees while also keeping an eye on the dog or holding your toddler nephew's hand. Your heart rate is steady, possibly slightly elevated due to mild exercise. You're at your best interpersonally, intelligently and emotionally.

Flight and fight: Now imagine that a bear comes out from the trees and heads towards you. Your chatter will stop. Your face will go flat, and your eyes will fix on the bear, not on the trees or flowers. Your heart will race, muscles tense and your body will prepare to run (flight) if you have time, or fight. Please note the order of that – *flight* then *fight*. Now, if you're thinking, 'I know/live with children who just do fight' then stay with me. I understand from my son that the type of bear (black, brown, polar) depends on which course of action is most likely to work in these circumstances!

Freeze: Now imagine that the bear is upon you – neither running nor taking flight worked and you are about to be mauled to death. You will enter a state of freeze in which having had tense muscles and fast beating heart, you will now have floppy muscles and your entire system will slow down. Blood will be directed from your extremities (arms, legs) towards your vital organs and you will be flooded with acetylcholine to numb any pain. Just to complicate things, there is also a mobilized form of freeze demonstrated by the rabbit in the headlights, where our muscles stay stiff and still, ready to move to flight or fight as soon as danger has passed.

When we perceive danger, our bodies mobilize. The sympathetic nervous system kicks in, increases adrenaline and heart rate and sends blood faster around the body to deliver oxygen so that we can run or fight. We try to run first but if that fails, we then move to fight. Perhaps if our trauma history has presented our nervous system with evidence that there is nowhere to run or that running doesn't work, we will drop through this stage further down our polyvagal ladder. This is where we're at if we become violent...thinking brain diminished, pumped and perceiving danger. If this progresses further into a sense of life threat, we go into freeze – again, if our trauma histories tell us that taking flight and fighting doesn't work, we may be predisposed to entering freeze when any form of fear is perceived.

From any of these danger states, we return to safe and social, not only when the body perceives that life threat or danger has passed but in the presence of connection to another (Poole Heller, *The Wisdom of Trauma Webinar*. 2021). How often has a child you live or work with had an experience where their physical environment was safe but relational connection was absent? How long were they down their ladders all alone?

This model is helpful because it helps us to frame aggression in terms of where a child is on their ladder but also in trying to create the flight-safety experiences that prevent them going into fight in the first place. Because it helps us understand our functional limitations as we drop further down our ladder, our interventions can be more targeted. Anything involving lots of words or rationale is wasted or escalatory on someone in fight because what they hear is limited and their thinking brain is offline. Use of body language and tone of voice are much more effective.

Acknowledgements

Sally

Thank you to my nearest and dearest for your love, kindness and fun. I am a better person for having you in my life. Thank you to my friends for the swims, dog walks, café chats, knitting natter and horsing around. Thank you to my work family for being amazing and making the best of everything, and to JKP for your long-lasting vision and humour.

Thank you to all the parents and carers I've met along the way, for travelling alongside me with such grit and generosity. You offer incredible care and commitment to the children in your lives.

Thank you to Carly for your partnership on this mammoth project and for your friendship and determination, and for all the sweary laughs. You live acceptance and that's a wonderful thing.

A special thank you to G. I'm looking forward to happy times by the sea with you. I think we deserve it.

Carly

First, to Sally for taking a mad leap of faith in asking me to join her in this collaboration. Our love of lists and swearing is the glue that binds us together. To Mum and Dad, Steve and Rosie Humphries, I love you. Sorry about the swearin'. Thank you, along with Margaret and Brian Kingswood, for so much support with my studies over the years. Thank you to my sisters, Sarah and Lauren, who always tell me they are proud. I hope I give you good reason to be. To the rest of my fam, Jimmy Whizz, Lewis 'Uncle Blook' and all my fun creatures, Liam, Bear, Lily and Lynx, for the tonic you are. Endless dollops of thanks to the following friends, our network of incredible supporters, without which we would not have withstood the tides of challenge, who cheered the wins with us and held us through losses: Sally and Jean-Phi Petit, your name is small, but your hearts are wide. Team Tamblyn, Team Wallowski and Tracy Humphries, Team Coomes, Team Francis, Team Arnold, Sarah Whitcombe-Avery, Lauren Avery, Joe (nickname sadly omitted) and Henna (Snotface) Mears and Team Addicott. You loved us well and I love you right back. Love and thanks to our wonderful neighbour, Stuart Gregory, who has never once moaned about the noise and always treasured our children. More recently, massive thanks to Nathalie and Gabriel Parry and Rich Astley for the support you have shown to us and our children, for steak nights, dogs, football and silliness.

Thank you to some amazing, dedicated youth leaders, Gav and Sharon Williams and Sally Evans and to our church family who supported and prayed. Thank you to some bloody good social workers, Lucy Day, Tarlie Walker and Suz Staples, your support was always on point and your ability to empathize and advocate for every member of our family was utterly refreshing. Huge thanks to Jenny Turner and Natalie Roberts, two kick-ass mummas who kindly read the first draft of this book in super-quick time and gave such helpful feedback. Thank you to my muses along the way who inspired me in my journey and wore your belief for me right on your sleeves: John Barnes, Liza Lomax, Joy Hasler, Micha Douglas, Anna Binnie-Dawson and Alison Keith. To my gorgeous PIC, Fred Lacey, thank you for always smelling beautiful and being there with a hug. With gratitude to two precious women whose strength and love for me was such that I still had some to hold on to when they left this world: Granny Jones (Edith Ellen Jones) and my friend, Diane Sanders.

Thank you to all the incredible families over the years who have shared their stories with me. To brave children and equally brave parents, carers, aunties, uncles, grandparents. Thank you especially to those whose stories you have allowed me to share in this book. To Lisa Kingswood, our little 'un who chose us as her family against the odds and for being the best teacher I ever had. To Noah and Hope, for sharing your parents, especially your Mama Chicken, with so many other children. You are both a marvel and I really wish there was a GCSE in kindness because you'd both be getting A*s/9s depending on how old the person reading this is. You are my happy place (most of the time), and you make me do better. Finally, to my best friend, David (Des) Kingswood. Thank you for your love and support, which is endless, if not sometimes annoying. Doing life with you is ace. Thank you for the sense of humour we share (where would we be without it?!), the adventures, and always driving.

Endnotes

1   Brown, B. (2021) *Atlas of the Heart*. New York, NY: Penguin Random House LLC.

2   Golding, K. (2014) Connection before correction: Supporting parents to meet the challenges of children who have been traumatised within their early parenting environments. *Children Australia*, 40(2): 1–8.

3   Eagleman, D. (2016) *The Brain: The Story of You*. Edinburgh: Canongate.

4   Brown, B. (2021) *Atlas of the Heart*. New York, NY: Penguin Random House LLC.

5   Yehuda, R *et al* (2005). Transgenerational Effects of Posttraumatic Stress Disorder in Babies of Mothers Exposed to the World Trade Center Attacks during Pregnancy. *Journal of Clinical Endocrinology & Metabolism*, DOI:110.1210/jc.2005-0550.

6   Hughes, D.A. (2009) *Attachment-Focused Parenting: Effective Strategies to Care for Children*. New York, NY: W.W. Norton.

7   Hughes, D.A., Golding, K. and Hudson, J. (2019) *Healing Relational Trauma with Attachment-Focused Interventions: Dyadic Developmental Psychotherapy with Children and Families*. New York, NY: W.W. Norton.

8   Hughes, D. A.; Golding, K. S. & Hudson, J. (2019) Healing relational trauma with attachment-focused interventions. NY: Norton.

9   Hart, A. (2015) *MY BRAIN – Why Dinosaur Brain Can Be Sooooooo Bossy!* Alison Hart.

10 Greene, R. (2021) *The Explosive Child: A New Approach for Understanding and Parenting Easily Frustrated, Chronically Inflexible* (sixth edition). New York, NY: Harper.

11 Brooks, R. (2020) *The Trauma and Attachment Aware Classroom: A Practical Guide to Supporting Children Who Have Encountered Trauma and Adverse Childhood Experiences*. London and Philadelphia, PA: Jessica Kingsley Publishers.

12 Holt, S. (2015) Post-separation fathering and domestic abuse: Challenges and contradictions. *Child Abuse Review*, 24(3): 210–222.

13 Morrison, F. (2015) 'All over now?' The ongoing relational consequences of domestic abuse through children's contact arrangements. *Child Abuse Review*, 24(4): 274–284.

14 Holt, S. (2011) Domestic abuse and child contact: Positioning children in the decision-making process. *Childcare in Practice*, 17(4): 327–346.

15 Kübler-Ross, E. and Kessler, D. (2005) *On Grief and Grieving: Finding the Meaning of Grief Through the Five Stages of Loss*. New York, NY: Scribner.

16   Siegel, D.J. (1999) *The Developing Mind*. New York, NY: Guilford.
17   Porges, S.W. (2011) *The Polyvagal Theory: Neurophysiological Foundations of Emotions, Attachment, Communication, and Self-Regulation*. New York, NY: W.W. Norton.